# *Technology for the School Librarian*

# Technology for the School Librarian

## Theory and Practice

*William O. Scheeren*

 LIBRARIES UNLIMITED

AN IMPRINT OF ABC-CLIO, LLC
Santa Barbara, California • Denver, Colorado • Oxford, England

**Library of Congress Cataloging-in-Publication Data**

Scheeren, William O.
    Technology for the school librarian : theory and practice / William O. Scheeren.
        p. cm.
    Includes bibliographical references and index.
    ISBN 978-1-59158-900-6 (acid-free paper) — ISBN 978-1-59158-901-3 (ebook) 1. School libraries—Information technology. 2. Internet in school libraries. 3. Library Web sites. 4. Digital libraries. 5. Libraries—Special collections—Computer network resources. I. Title.
    Z675.S3S259 2010
    025.042—dc22        2009051922

ISBN: 978-1-59158-900-6
E-ISBN: 978-1-59158-901-3

14  13  12  11  10    1 2 3 4 5

This book is also available on the World Wide Web as an eBook.
Visit www.abc-clio.com for details.

ABC-CLIO, LLC
130 Cremona Drive, P.O. Box 1911
Santa Barbara, California 93116-1911

This book is printed on acid-free paper ∞
Manufactured in the United States of America

# Contents

# 1

# *School Libraries in the "Bad Old Days"*

## WHY COMPUTER TECHNOLOGY IS IMPORTANT

For school librarians entering the field in the past twenty years, there is little or no recollection of the school library without computer technology. This is a fact, but within this library there are widely varying levels of technology hardware, software, and expertise. The use of technology in the school library is a given among the practitioners of today, but the questions of "what," "how," and "who" as they relate to school library technology are ones that must be addressed—and if we do not address them in a satisfactory way, the job of the school librarian, and even the existence of the school library as we know it, could be in danger.

Am I trying to alarm school librarians? I am, and I hope that I succeed, because our future as a profession is at stake. One has only to read the newspapers (something that is still important!) and to watch the media portray the ways that people have changed their information-seeking behavior to realize that this is true. The media collectively says that today we are a society founded on information. If that is so—and there really is no reason to doubt that it is—shouldn't the library, and in our case the school library, be at the very center of this search for information? One would think so, but too often school librarians are presented as being out of the "new" information loop. Recently I was able to hear a member of a local school board say that there really wasn't any need for a budget for school libraries—or, for that matter, any need for school librarians—because everything the students need as far as information is concerned is available on the Internet for free. For all the power and information the Internet has given us and our students, using the Internet as a replacement for the school library is just wrongheaded.

How do we counter these statements? We become leaders and experts in technology in our school libraries. How many of us have the level of expertise in the technology to be leaders in our schools? Just out of curiosity, how many of us still keep and maintain a hard-copy shelf list because we just do not trust the electronic database not to crash and instantly erase all the information about our collection? Don't be shy—put your hands right up. How many of you know that it would be good for your students to be able to access library materials remotely but don't know how to make the case for such capabilities to your technology coordinator or your administration? If you answered yes to either of the last two questions, you need to take a hard look at your technology skills, at the technology available in your library, and at your current capacity for being a leader in the field of educational technology.

So far, we have addressed the shortcomings in technology and technology expertise that could be disastrous for the school librarian. Am I saying that the role of the school librarian has changed to a point at which we are "information managers," rather than school librarians? Although a case could be made for this, that is not what I am saying. Rather, I wish to emphasize that if the school librarian does not add technology leadership and technology expertise to the litany of skills he or she now has, then the field will pass librarians by, and we will be less and less relevant in our field and in our schools.

## HOW TECHNOLOGY HAS CHANGED
## THE SCHOOL LIBRARY

How has technology changed the school library and the school librarian? Go back about forty years and consider how the school library typically worked. Forty years ago, the first of the baby boomers were completing high school and moving on to college or into the workforce. In many cases, smaller schools were overwhelmed with more students than they could handle, and the first school consolidations began to take place. The advent of Sputnik in 1957 caused increased emphasis on mathematics and science in American schools, but in some ways schools were much the same in 1969 as they had been 100 years before. Take, for example, the school year. In 1969, as well as today, the school year is based on the farm cycle, with nine months of school and three months off in the summer. The school year was like that in 1869, was like that in 1969, and remains like that today.

In many ways, the school library of 1969 might look very familiar to us. It would have books, magazines, and perhaps some other types of print media. In the late 1960s, there would probably be a nascent audiovisual collection: films, filmstrips, and records, available for teacher use. These audiovisual materials were the extent of technology in the school library, except for the librarian's typewriter, which turned out endless catalog cards for filing. Occasionally, the school library was also home to the record players and projectors needed for use of the library's audiovisual technology.

Physically, the school library would probably closely resemble today's facility. Some amount of restricted access led into an essentially square room with tables and chairs for students. Book stacks lined the walls and perhaps extended from the wall perpendicularly, if the collection was large enough. Magazines and newspapers were available. In the center of the facility was the charging desk that was the domain of the librarians and their student assistants. And don't forget one thing: the card catalog, that set of drawers with cards allegedly created to help find books but really created to torture the unwary student or teacher. Who among us can forget those helpful words of the school librarian: "Look it up in the catalog!"

Let's jump forward forty years to the typical school library of 2009. The room is still square, and the books and book stacks are still there, as are the magazines and newspapers. Perhaps the biggest difference between the school library of 1969 and that of 2009 is the computers you'll see—and the absence of the card catalog. Still, though, we hear: "Look it up . . . "

What is described above is the usual level of technology available in school libraries. The question then arises: how much is enough technology? and even, for some: how much is too much? If we were to ask our students, they would say you can never have enough technology. Their parents would probably agree, to a point, but would advocate technology that would assist their children's learning. The school administration and governing body would probably say that whatever technology can be paid for is a sufficient amount. The school librarian might cap technology at the limit of what can be maintained and used.

It is interesting to note that several of the Keith Curry Lance studies showed a similar conclusion, regardless of the state: technology extends the reach of an effective library program, with evidence showing that schools with effective technology programs have more effective library programs. Curry Lance further stated that the best school libraries were integrated into computer networks, and provided remote access to library resources to their students.

## LEVELS OF TECHNOLOGY ACCEPTANCE

Kochtanek and Matthews (2002, 7) in their work dealing with technology in all types of libraries, identify four different levels of acceptance of technology among librarians. Although their conclusions relate not just to school librarians, we can identify those among us at the different levels of acceptance.

The first level of acceptance Kochtanek and Matthews identify as the "bleeding edge." Librarians in this category are far out ahead of the pack and are eager to implement any new type of library technology application as soon as it is released. Along with the desire to lead, they want state-of-the-art hardware as soon as it is released. School librarians at this bleeding edge of technology are the envy of many of us, because they always seem to have the resources at their disposal to move forward with library technology.

Some school librarians do not envy those at the bleeding edge. These are the school librarians who are generally satisfied with the level of technology in their libraries and have a great deal of trepidation about moving forward. Worse, their students, their parents, and their administration are often comparing them to those at the bleeding edge, to their embarrassment and chagrin.

Being at the bleeding edge of technology is not always an unalloyed positive. The possibility of buying technology that is inefficient or rapidly out of date is a real possibility. Furthermore, there is always technology that promises much and delivers little. As a cautionary tale, we should keep in mind the teaching machines of the 1960s and 1970s. School districts may still have storage areas full of teaching machines, a technology that promised much and delivered little. Many districts were a bit skeptical of the proliferation of computers, asking if they were the second coming of the teaching machines.

The second level of technology acceptance in the school library, according to Kochtanek and Matthews, is the "leading edge." School libraries in this category are still considered to be leaders in the use of technology, but not to the extent of those at the bleeding edge. Typically, school libraries in this category are eager to move forward with technological innovation but are willing to hang back enough to see how successful these innovations will be. These are the school librarians that are not using beta versions of software or the latest operating systems as soon as they are released, and whose libraries are not demonstration sites for the most advanced library technology applications.

Instead, people on the leading edge carefully evaluate new technology. Once a technology has been proven in the field, they are ready to move. Librarians at the leading edge seldom have a storage area filled with outdated technology that never quite served its purpose or never quite worked right. School librarians at the leading edge are largely supported in their technology initiatives by their administration, because they seldom make foolish purchases, seldom waste funds, and generally keep their school libraries leaders in technology.

The third level of technology acceptance is where the vast majority of school librarians fall, for better or worse. This is the level known as being in the wedge. They are not risk-takers, and are satisfied to be in this wedge area. These school librarians report to their administrators that the level of technology in their libraries is the same as most schools in their area. This response, this approach, could also be called the "safe" approach. The theory is that if you never take a risk, you will never make a mistake. A visitor to a school library in the wedge would certainly see an online catalog and online databases, but a limited number of computers for students. The school librarian is not one of the leaders in technology in the school.

The fourth and final level of technology acceptance is known as the trailing edge. In World War II flying parlance, such librarians would have been known as "tail-end Charlies." School librarians in this category have to be dragged kicking and screaming to accept any kind of technology in their school libraries. It is not a matter of money, but more the lack of inertia, or the outright unwillingness, to move forward. These are the school librarians who still have their shelf list cards because they think the system may crash, causing all of their data to be lost.

The librarians on the trailing edge always have an excuse for why they haven't moved forward with library technology. "I only have ____ years until retirement." "I'm too old to learn all of this technology stuff." "My administration won't let me spend any money." "I still like to hold that book in my hands." We have all heard these excuses, and each time one is overcome there are others waiting. Librarians at the trailing edge rarely change: they will not move forward with technology, no matter what. So who will be in danger if they do not move forward with technology? It goes without saying that those school librarians in the trailing edge are at risk—as well they should be. And the school librarians in the wedge are at risk, and don't understand why. As we move into the twenty-first century, it is not enough to be in the crowd as a school librarian. We, as a profession, have to be leaders in technology. We have to provide our students with the highest-quality library services available, and that means being a leader in technology. The technology train for school librarians is leaving the station: if you aren't on it, you'll be run over!

## THE EVOLUTION OF TECHNOLOGY IN THE SCHOOL LIBRARY

In this section, we outline how new technologies have affected the operation of the school library. Not all these things have happened in all school libraries, and neither have they taken place at the same pace in all school libraries. Furthermore, school libraries have rarely been the leaders in the implementation of these technologies. Academic libraries, and to a lesser degree public libraries, have generally had that role. Why? Most school libraries are open during the fall and spring semesters, but closed all summer. Consider that the typical school library is almost exclusively curriculum-driven, without the other missions carried out by academic libraries (such as the research agenda of the faculty) and public libraries (meeting the recreational needs of patrons). It has often been easy for school librarians to place less emphasis on technology than have their counterparts in academic and public libraries.

In other cases, the duties of the school librarian have precluded their taking the time to learn and implement technology innovations. This can be a slippery slope on which to embark, but elementary school librarians scheduled to teach every period of the day as prep-time relief for a classroom teacher are severely limited in the time available for even the most mundane library administration tasks.

## Circulation Systems

Although technology applications did not begin to appear in school libraries until after 1980, as a general rule, automated circulation systems begin to appear in academic libraries some period before that. Circulation has always been viewed as a repetitive task that some think can be accomplished by nonprofessionals. Academic libraries (and all libraries, for that matter) have viewed the automation of circulation as laborsaving, and a natural outgrowth of using college computer systems.

Circulation was also generally the first library function in the school library to be automated, but it occurred considerably later than in academic libraries. This was so because school libraries rarely had the in-house computer systems and expertise required to accomplish this. For many schools through the mid-1970s, total computing capability was computer time leased—perhaps one or two hours at a time—from a local college or industry to perform business functions. There just was not the expertise or capability to automate the school library's circulation system. That had to wait for the proliferation of microcomputer technology into school libraries.

## Security Systems

Many school librarians would not consider security systems to be technology in the most modern sense of the term, but a strong case can be made that a security system is technology. Not only is it technology, but it was the first technology that many school librarians had the opportunity to use. Security systems filled a practical purpose and were approved by school administrations and school boards for one simple reason—they saved money! As security systems became more prevalent in the 1970s, school librarians, especially those in high schools, found they were typically saving between 80% and 90% in lost book costs. School boards and administrators quickly saw the financial savings and became strong proponents of security systems.

Not all school libraries were designed to take best advantage of security systems. Some aesthetically pleasing features of school libraries, such as multiple entrances and exits and outside access, can make school library security systems less effective, but their ability to reduce book losses continue to make them near "must-haves" in the twenty-first-century school library.

### Cataloging, Library Systems, and MARC

In pretechnology days, the cataloging of materials was a major undertaking in the school library. Cataloging was laborious—and, some school librarians with a bent toward cataloging would posit, has its own artistry. Perhaps, but cataloging was often an area that received less than its due share emphasis before technology came to school libraries.

Few veterans in the profession can forget how beneficial it was to receive books from jobbers that included catalog cards. It was not always neat Dewey Decimal Classification System or Library of Congress cataloging, but it fulfilled the primary purpose of cataloging—allowing books to be found on the shelves. Although the best possible cataloging was always the goal, sometimes less than that was acceptable for purposes of getting books into circulation, and allowing them to be found on the shelves.

The advent of the technology that allowed for automated cataloging happened first in the academic arena, for many of the reasons outlined above. Academic libraries generally took advantage of their on-campus computer systems to automate the cataloging function. Furthermore, they had the personnel with the cataloging expertise to make the system work, in contrast to the school library, where even best-case scenarios had perhaps only two librarians to perform all functions in the school library, including library skills instruction. As was the case with automated circulation systems, proliferation had to wait for the widespread use of the personal computer.

### Personal Computers

Computers have been with us since the 1940s. Early computers were invented to automate repetitive tasks, such as the formulation of artillery trajectories. The first practical computer that did just this was ENIAC, built at the University of Pennsylvania. These early computers operated using a combination of vacuum tubes and circuits to perform their calculations. Without going through a lengthy history of the development of the computer, keep in mind the evolution of a device that filled an entire building with less computing power than is contained in today's personal digital assistants (PDAs). As a matter of fact, the United States put men in space with less computing power than an iPod has.

Two developments eventually brought us to the personal computer as we know it. The first was the development of the transistor at Bell Labs in 1947, for which William Shockley, John Bardeen, and Walter Brattain received a Nobel Prize. The second was the development of the silicon chip, which made the personal computer in its present incantation possible. We are not in the business of trying to determine the most significant inventions in history, but the personal computer would certainly have a high rank. This is equally true for its impact on the school library and the school librarian. Although automation in the school library was possible using mainframes and minicomputers, it was not practical. The personal computer, however, changed that.

As we move forward in our continuum of computer technology in the school library, we can recall the first stand-alone personal computers in a school district. They looked good, but what could be done on them? Many summer workshops were spent writing simple BASIC programs that calculated such things as speeding fines for drivers' education. In those days floppy disks were just that, and we used a paper punch to punch a notch on the disk to make it double-sided, to increase capacity and to save money. For school librarians, the big advance was to be able to use an application such as Appleworks to actually automate some library functions.

One of the early goals of technology, and not just in libraries or businesses, was to create what was optimistically known as a paperless society. This goal was as much a pipe dream as were the expectations of Thomas Watson, chairman of IBM, 1943, regarding the need for computers: "I think there is a world market for maybe five computers" (Strohmeyer). Not only do we not have a paperless society, but the explosion in the amount of information available has geometrically increased the amount of paper used.

The evolution of the personal computer suddenly made it possible for school libraries to automate functions such as circulation, cataloging, and the use of the library catalog. Closely tied to these innovations was the invention of easy-to-use, easy-to-maintain networks. Without these networks, it would not have been possible to provide practical public online catalogs. It was wondrous to use that first library system in which one could see items in nearly real time when they were added to the system, searching for all the books on a particular subject to see whether they were checked out. We are miles beyond that today, but in our minds, we still should see that school librarian who keeps the shelf list up to date because "the system might go down."

### Audiovisual Equipment and Materials

Through the "bad old days" down to today, the school library has frequently been the home of audiovisual hardware and materials. For many years this meant film projectors, filmstrip projectors, record players, cassette players, and perhaps even videotape equipment. In addition, the school librarian maintained a store of spare parts and bulbs to answer that inevitable call: "This thing won't work!" A certain level of repair expertise was also part of the job description. Although the media and the hardware have changed over the years, this function is generally still a part of the school librarian's duties.

Today, instead of film projectors, school librarians distribute DVD players. Computer projectors, located in most classrooms, are now used to stream video available from commercial sources. As we look at different methods of delivery, it may well be that what was formerly available in the school library or in a support facility may be available electronically. This is an area that will bear watching, for it has the potential to significantly change the operation of the school library.

### Internet and Electronic Resources

We have discussed the impact that the invention and proliferation of personal computers have had on the school librarian. A logical outgrowth of the technology, and an innovation that has had a profound impact on the school library, is the Internet, along with the use of digital resources. This is one of the easiest areas in which to contrast the past with the present. In the past—certainly prior to 1985—neither the Internet, to any practical degree, nor digital resources, existed.

Prior to the use of the Internet and electronic resources, what was available to students in the school library was simple: books and magazines. Books were located using the card catalog, and students took notes on the information needed—or, if they were fortunate, were able to photocopy material. If they were using an encyclopedia and another student was using the volume needed, they simply had to wait. The use of magazines was also straightforward. A student would search the *Reader's Guide to Periodical Literature* for articles relating to a certain topic and then determine whether their library had the magazine desired. If not, it was back to the *Reader's Guide*. While disarmingly simple, the process was little changed since the advent of school libraries.

School librarians recognized early that this was an area that could be significantly improved by technology. One of the earliest attempts to use technology to improve student access to resources came in the form of a product named Info-Trak. This product allowed users to search a microfilm file that was supplied monthly to find magazine articles, and then to view the article on microfiche. It was no longer necessary for the school library to have paper copies of all indexed magazines.

As revolutionary as this was, it was the introduction of online searching using services such as Bibliography Reference Service (BRS) or Dialog that really broadened the availability of resources. These computer-based services were far from easy to use, and searching remained the purview of librarians. In many cases, school librarians were required to take college courses in the searching techniques required to use these databases. The use of BRS and Dialog required the use of a database thesaurus, and the use of the databases required per minute payment. This intermediate step was only a prelude to . . .

. . . the Internet! It is difficult to overestimate the impact and value the Internet has had on information-seeking behavior in the school library. From its earliest days as a terminal-based network using Mosaic to its ubiquitous graphical-user interface, the Internet has significantly changed the ease with which data could be accessed, in ever-increasing amounts. This significant change has not all been for the good. The huge amount of information available on the Internet has made it incumbent on the school librarian to thoroughly and completely teach how to evaluate information. Too often students use search engines using general search terms such as "World War II" or "Shakespeare" and then are flummoxed when the search yields 10 million or more results.

The nature of the Internet as an unmediated network has resulted in large numbers of Web pages with invalid, incorrect, or biased information. Too often our students take this information at face value, saying, in effect, "If it's on the Internet, it must be true."

Collateral to the Internet is the use of electronic databases, which use the Internet for access but provide information that is always credible. With training, they allow users to find exactly the information they need. These databases can be general, or extremely specialized. For example, many of the general periodical indexes allow users to access the full text of 2,000+ magazines dating back as far as ten years, or even longer. This stands in stark contrast to the days of the *Reader's Guide* and hard-copy magazines.

Other databases are very narrow in their coverage. These are specialized databases that are designed specifically for college students; others are specifically for elementary school students. One of the major issues that school librarians face with relation to electronic databases is their cost. One of the innovations that will be discussed in more detail later in the book is such participatory databases as Wikipedia. Such free databases based on the contributions of users will have an impact on the school library.

### Web 2.0

Web 2.0 is a group of social networking applications that have since their inception been the purview of the students rather than the teachers. This seems to be changing as schools and school librarians are adapting such Web 2.0 applications as blogs, wikis, podcasts, and virtual conferencing to educational use. In some ways the most difficult task the school librarian faces when using these applications is convincing parents and school administration that there are educationally viable reasons for using these Web 2.0 applications.

What is the future for school librarians and technology? Only time will tell, but one fact is inescapable: school librarians must be leaders in educational technology if they are to remain viable in the schools of the future.

Chapter 1 is an introduction to the broad scope of technology in the school library. The "bad old days" of the school library without technology were described, and a description of the possibilities of technology in the school library was presented. The point was made that it is important for school librarians to become leaders in technology if they are to retain their relevance. Chapter 2 will be a detailed examination of the technology skills that school librarians must possess to continue being the hub of learning in the school.

## RESOURCES

American Library Association. "AASL Information Power Action Research Project." AASL. www.ala.org/ala/mgrps/divs/aasl/aaslproftools/informationpower/informationpower .cfm (accessed January 11, 2009).

Borgman, Christine. "From Acting Locally to Thinking Globally: A Brief History of Library Automation." *The Library Quarterly*, 67, 215–249.

Burke, John J. *Neal-Schuman Library Technology Companion: A Basic Guide for Library Staff.* New York: Neal-Schuman, 2004.

Doggett, Sandra L. *Beyond the Book: Technology Integration into the Secondary School Library Media Curriculum.* Englewood, CO: Libraries Unlimited, 2000.

Herrin, Mark. "10 Reasons Why the Internet Is No Substitute for a Library." ALA. www.ala.org/ala/alonline/resources/selectedarticles/10reasonswhy.cfm (accessed January 12, 2009).

Johnson, Doug. "Are Libraries (and Librarians) Headed toward Extinction?" *Teacher Librarian* 2:24–27.

Johnson, Doug. "Why Do We Need Libraries When We Have the Internet?" *Knowledge Quest* 27(1). www.doug-johnson.com/dougwri/why-do-we-libraries-when-we-have-the-internet.html (accessed January 14, 2009).

Jurkowski, Odin L. *Technology and the School Library: A Comprehensive Guide for Media Specialists and Other Educators*. Lanham, MD: Scarecrow, 2006.

Kochtanek, Thomas R., and Joseph R. Matthews. *Library Information Systems: From Library Automation to Distributed Information Access Solutions*. Westport, CT: Libraries Unlimited, 2002.

Kohn, John M., Ann L. Kelsey, and Keith Michael Fields. *Planning for Integrated Systems and Technologies: A How-To-Do-It Manual for Librarians*. New York: Neal-Schuman, 2001.

Lance, Keith Curry. "What Research Tells Us About the Importance of School Libraries." White House Conference on School Libraries. www.imls.gov/news/events/whitehouse_2.shtm#kcl (accessed July 15, 2009).

"Library Technology Awareness Resources." Library Technology Awareness. www.users.muohio.edu/burkejj/techawareness.html (accessed January 12, 2009).

Odlyzko, Andrew. "Silicon Dreams and Silicon Bricks: The Continuing Evolution of Libraries." http://hdl.handle.net/2142/8137 (accessed January 12, 2009).

"School Libraries History." Internet School Library Media Center (ISLMC) School Library History. http://falcon.jmu.edu/~ramseyil/libhistory.htm (accessed January 11, 2009).

Strohmeyer, Robert. "The 7 Worst Tech Predictions of All Time." http://tech.msn.com/news/articlepcw.aspx?cp-documentid=16829041 (accessed August 3, 2009).

Williams, Brad. *We're Getting Wired, We're Going Mobile, What's Next?: Fresh Ideas for Educational Technology Planning*. Eugene, OR: ISTE, 2004.

# QUESTIONS FOR RESEARCH AND DISCUSSION

1. In Chapter 1, a school board member was noted as saying that school libraries do not need books because everything is available on the Internet. That school board member also believes that everything on the Internet is free. Is that person correct in both of the statements? Why, or why not? Your response to this should be research-based, citing several sources to support your answer.

2. The students in school now are sometimes known as digital natives because they have grown up with technology. The implication is that they can do almost anything using technology. From your experience in a school library, is this true? If you believe it to be, comment on how they view the technology that is available in your school library. If you believe it to be false, comment on the technology skills they appear to lack. Examine research that is available on this question, and determine whether it agrees with your perception.

3. What is your view as to the best place your school library should be with relation to the adoption of technology? Should you be at the bleeding edge, on the leading edge, or in the wedge? Based on your experience in your school library, justify your answer. You may want to discuss this issue with other librarians in your district, as well as with building- and district-level administrators.

4. A number of advances were discussed in the chapter as regards library technology. Which one had the greatest impact on the school library? Describe why you believe as you do, and back your response with research. Which had the least impact? Again, although you will include your personal opinion here, conduct research to support your response.

5. One of the greatest issues facing the school librarian as regards technology is the lack of IT support. Is this a problem in your school? If so, what can you do to ameliorate the problem? Compare the level of IT support in your district with the level of IT support in an industry or business in your area. Do trends emerge?

6. Examine three or more online sources to find definitions of technology. Use the results of your research to come to your own definition of technology. Ask some of your colleagues to define technology, and evaluate whether their definitions differ significantly from your own.

# 2

# *Technology Skills for School Librarians*

Determining what technology skills a school librarian should possess is one of the most important measures in determining how effective the school library will be in the twenty-first century. It is important to determine the skills needed by the school librarians as well as how the skills are acquired and how the skills are maintained and updated.

One of the most erroneous statements about the preparation of school librarians extant is that (1) they bring all the technology skills they will need into library school because they are digital natives and (2) the coursework in library school will provide them all of the technology skills they need.

Both of these statements are spectacularly erroneous. First, while the students, considered digital natives, do possess many technology skills, their technology skills are eclectic at best. They can create Facebook accounts and download music, but they cannot organize files in the Windows environment. They can use digital cameras and download pictures to their computers, but they cannot set up headers and footers in a word processing program. These digital natives can program a cell phone or a VCR but have no idea how to create formulas that will unleash the power of a spreadsheet program. Unfortunately this is often the hodgepodge of technology skills prospective school librarians bring with them to library school.

The second erroneous statement is that library school will provide prospective school librarians all of the technology skills they will need. If this were true, it would solve the entire issue. Unfortunately, however, the technology skills taught to prospective school librarians vary as widely as the technology skills the students bring with them to library school. Very few of the school library programs have discrete courses dealing with technology, and if they do, they deal with specific applications or provide a general introduction to productivity software.

Is this bad? Not in itself when compared with other programs that provide instruction in technology only within other courses, but instruction in specific software or in the use of productivity software only scratches the surface of the software skills that will be required of school librarians in the twenty-first century.

Let us settle one issue once and for all. The preparation programs that will prepare school librarians to work in our schools of the future must prepare them as thoroughly in technology as in the skills traditionally required of school librarians. To fail to do so does a great disservice not only to the school librarians but also to the students they will work with. Furthermore, school districts looking forward on behalf of their students will not employ those school librarians who do not have the necessary level of technology skills.

## THE ROLE OF THE SCHOOL LIBRARIAN

The issue of the technology skills required of the school librarian was analyzed by Carrie Lowe in an online publication from 2001. The author posits that librarians are the original information specialists or information managers. This position cannot be overemphasized despite a significant level of opposition from old-line school librarians. The old liners say we are librarians and even using the word information denigrates the role and idea of the school librarian. This is seen all too often in the school librarian whose instructional program consists of two things: book selection and reading to the students. These are great parts of a school library instructional program, but there are a myriad of other information skills that are equally important to the student. Failing to adapt to these information skills requirements might be malpractice by the school librarian.

In 1997, University of Nebraska researcher Gary Hartzell (1997) recognized the importance of information and technology skills to the school librarian. He saw the failure of the school librarian to be a participant in the decisions that affected technology not only at the district or building level but even in the school library itself. He also found that few, if any, schools of education focused on the importance of the library and of information in the learning process. Is it any wonder, in light of these findings, that the school librarian can become superfluous and, when budget cutting occurs, unemployed?

Hartzell's findings with regard to school librarians and technology, even at that early date, had great implications for the "traditional" school librarian. While not denying the value of books and other print material, it emphasized the role of the school librarian as information managers or specialists and as educators. This research also presented what Hartzell called "guiding principles" (Hartzell 1997) for the school librarian as we move further into the twenty-first century. Each of these principles presented have implications for the level and type of technology skills that will be required for the school librarian to be a viable force in American education.

- There are no walls associated with school libraries. The power of technology has made this a truism. Once limited by a collection within four walls, technology has made the expectations greater. Students expect, and deserve, access to library materials twenty-four hours a day, seven days a week, from any location. The means that the technology-savvy school librarian must provide their patrons access to library resources from home. Anything less is not acceptable.
- Even more than in previous years the school librarian must be flexible. This is not just Hartzell's view; it was put forth in the ALA Publication *Information Power: Building Partnerships for Learning.* The reality of the situation is that if you are not the most flexible person in your building, you are not flexible enough. You must be able to move seamlessly between the roles as teacher, instructional planner, information specialist, and program administrator.
- You must insure that your students are effective users of information. There can be no question that our society is an information-based society. For better or worse, we are no longer a society that makes things. What are the implications for our students as we move from a production-based society? It means that all students must be able to manipulate and use information because the manufacturing jobs that did not require the use of information simply no longer exist. One has only to travel through the Northeast and Midwest "rust belts" to see the truth of this. This now is the essence of the school librarian's task: to ensure that their students are ready for these information challenges.
- Information is everywhere and, as mentioned above, is central in our lives. Sometimes we, as well as our students, are shortsighted about this concept. Doing research is as important in the job search process as when researching a topic in the library. The whole concept that information is everywhere is key in the quest to ensure that our students are effective users of information.

Contrary to popular opinion, the proliferation of information in our society and the use of technology in our schools emphasize the need for library and technology in all of our schools. This statement brings us face-to-face with administrators or school board members who believe that technology and the Internet obviate the need for school libraries and librarians.

Over ten years ago the term "intermediation" was coined. The idea was that as technology became more advanced, users would require less assistance to use it. As we have seen, this is patently untrue. As technology has become more advanced, users require more, rather than less, assistance. One has only to observe student searches for information to see this. Students believe that Googling for information is the be-all and end-all of information seeking, regardless of the millions of matches the most basic search yields. Furthermore, without extensive mediation, students are unable to discriminate between good and bad sources. Rather than students requiring less assistance using more advanced technology, more assistance is required.

This brings us back to the skills related to technology that are required of the school librarian. These are still general, but as we move forward you will be able to see the meshing of these with more specific skills.

- Learn about technology. See what technology can do for your library and see how you can use the technology. This learning process must be ongoing and be an integral part of your professional development.
- Be involved with technology in your school. Be on the technology committee. Be on the strategic planning committee. It is easy to make excuses as to why you cannot, but you need to do these things and be a leader on these committees.

These steps are no longer optional. Failure to do these things is not only a disservice to your students but could cost you your job.

## COMPUTER SKILLS IN CONTEXT

When examining the technology skills a school librarian must have, consideration must be given to the context in which the skills will be used. For many years school librarians have worked mightily to avoid teaching library skills in isolation. Nothing was more deadly for students than coming to the library to "learn how to use the *Reader's Guide,*" no matter if the students were doing research at that time or not. The ability of the school librarian to plan and work with the classroom teacher to integrate information skills into the curriculum has eased this issue to a considerable degree, at least in secondary schools. This will be discussed in greater detail in Chapter 11.

The advent of technology has brought these issues to the table again. In some cases we have not even determined the role of technology and more specifically the role of the computer in education. Early on the use of computers involved programming and, as time passed, the use of productivity software. Just as we were more empowered through the integration of library skills into the curriculum, so will we be empowered as we integrate the use of technology and information skills into the curriculum. No longer should the computer be a "real powerful" typewriter.

As the use of technology has advanced, we still see those most involved with it as either business education teachers, mathematics teachers, or technology education teachers. These people all have some vested interest in the use of technology in education but are generally not specifically trained as school librarians are in the use and integration of information through technology into education. What are some technology competencies that might be relevant to the school library and librarian?

- Knowing the basic operation, terminology, and first echelon maintenance for technology equipment.
- Knowledge of computer-assisted programs.
- Knowledge of the impact of technology on careers, society, and our culture.
- Computer programming.

## SCHOOL LIBRARIES: AN UNDER-RESOURCED RESOURCE

A study completed in Canada in 2005 by David Coish (2005) echoed many of the conclusions reached earlier and reemphasized the need for technologically proficient school librarians in order for students to move forward in our information-based society. Some interesting highlights of the study included that 75 percent of school principals felt a majority of their teachers and school librarians had enough skill with technology to use computers for administrative purposes. Conversely, less than half the principals felt the majority of their teachers had the skills to effectively integrate computer applications into their instruction or to teach students how to use computers.

Coish found that as the number of school librarians in a school increased, the likelihood of technology applications incorporated into instruction increased. The implication here is that there is a strong correlation between having school librarians in schools and the use of specialized technology applications in instruction. It appears that if school librarians are thoroughly trained in the use of technology, they not only perform a valuable role in the educational process of students, but can act as mentors for their fellow teachers, assisting them in becoming more proficient in the use of technology.

The survey of the role of the school librarian and the technology skills they must possess is necessarily theoretical. It is necessary because a lack of a theoretical framework makes any conclusions about technology and the school library and the technology skills necessary for the twenty-first-century school librarian questionable.

# GENERAL TECHNOLOGY SKILLS

## *Introduction*

When we consider the technology skills needed by school librarians, be they general or specific, we have to consider where these librarians will learn these technology skills. As alluded to in Chapter 1 and earlier in this chapter, it is pretty obvious that technology skills are not being taught in many certification programs to preservice school librarians. Why is this when it is again obvious that technology skills are widely required for any school library position? Perhaps one or two explanations can be advanced. First, many library schools perpetuate some difference between "library science stuff" and "information science stuff." More traditional library science faculty members often see technology as a great divide that should rarely if ever be crossed. Second, many view the school library as one of the last bastions of traditional, print-oriented skills. Many in the profession are careful to refer to themselves as librarians, rather than information managers. It may also be that library schools with no full-time school library specialist on the faculty have no one to keep faculty members informed about new trends in school libraries. With no one assigned this role, it is likely the school is still admitting students who have chosen this field for many wrong reasons.

In a sense this is analogous to the prospective school librarian who responds to the question "Why did you want to become a librarian?" with the response "I love books and love to read." If that is a preservice school librarian's reason for entering the profession, they probably need to find a job in a bookstore because a love for reading is not a key skill for a school librarian. At any rate, technology skills are not being taught to any great degree in school library preservice programs: this must change.

## *Basic Technology Skills*

- Embrace Change. This is a basic corollary for school librarians. If you do not embrace change, particularly as it relates to technology, you will become as much of an anachronism as buggy whip manufacturers became with the advent of the automobile. This is not to say that all school librarians need to be on the so-called "bleeding edge" of technology all of the time, but the meaning is clear: get rid of that shelf list and move forward with technology. If you do not have a computer at home, get one. Get a cell phone and learn how to send text messages.

Buy a PDA and use it. Convert those precious vinyl LPs to digital and put them on your iPod (you have one, don't you?). In other words, get on the technology train. If you do not, it will run over you.

- Be Comfortable Online. Being comfortable online seems so basic that some might question this as being worthy of mention. It does, however, get right to the base of today's technology in the school library. Not only must you be able to use cataloging software and search databases, the technologically savvy school librarian must know and be able to use search engines more effectively than just using one-word general searches in Google. You must be able to evaluate the resources you find online. We all know that there are widespread bias and outright falsehoods on the Internet; you must be able to evaluate this mass of information. You must be able to work with e-mail much more than just sending a joke a day to your colleagues. You must overcome the fear that students using e-mail in school is bad and accept that there are good, cogent reasons for students to be able to communicate electronically in real time. To be more succinct, you must be as comfortable online as your students are.

- Be Able to Fix Things. A long-existing fable in the myths of information technology describes the help desk rep at (Dell, Apple, take your choice) who was contacted by a computer user who could not get their computer to turn on. The user and the help desk rep went through numerous checklists and steps to determine why the computer would not turn on, to no avail. Becoming progressively more frustrated, the help desk rep, on a whim, asked the user if the computer was plugged in. When the response was "ah, no" the exasperated help desk rep responded "Then you are too [expletive deleted] dumb to use a computer."

    Apocryphal? Probably, but what the military would call first echelon maintenance should be core skills for school librarians. When an entire bank of computers goes black right in the middle of the OPAC lesson, the first place you will want to look is at the power cable that has mysteriously been unplugged. The second place to look is for those pesky network cables that magically become unplugged. Sometimes these things happen maliciously, but much more often students will test you. Nothing deflates a sixth-grade jokester more rapidly than just plugging the plug back in and going on with the lesson.

    It is true about school libraries and school districts that there will be a limited number of Information Technology (IT) personnel available to maintain technology. In fact, school districts often have less than 10 percent of the number of personnel that industry would have to maintain the same number of computers. Furthermore, there is constant turnover in school district IT personnel because of the low pay. A second truism is that school districts will pay their head of IT less than a teacher, while that individual would make more than the superintendent if they were in industry. It is very frustrating for these underpaid and overworked people to receive a call from a harried school librarian reporting that all the computers in the library have gone down, only to arrive in the library and discover a playful student has pulled a plug or two. As a school librarian you should be able to put paper in printers and clear paper jams. Know how to use a wide variety of storage devices. In other words, be comfortable doing basic maintenance on the technology in your library.

- Be Willing and Able to Learn New Technologies. If you are to be a technology leader in your school, you must be able to learn new technologies, and you must be eager to do so. When your school receives new technology, you should be right there ready to learn about it, regardless if it will be specifically housed or used in the library. How you learn to use the technology is not important. Some people learn better by sitting down with the documentation and learning systematically, while others are more eclectic learners and would rather play with and experiment with the technology to learn how to use it. A bit of a caveat with this latter method is that sometimes experimenters do not realize all of the features or do not use all of the features of technology in the most effective way.

  - Perhaps one of the best ways to sharpen your skills with new technology is to do a workshop or training session for other librarians or teachers on either new hardware or software. This puts them in a nonthreatening environment in which they can thoroughly learn new technology and you can verify in your own mind your knowledge of the technology. Conducting staff development with technology for your teachers places you squarely in that leadership role! Training is wonderful! Unfortunately many school districts seem to think teachers can learn about technology without training. They are reminiscent of the characters in the movie *Field of Dreams:* "Build it and they will come," only they believe if you provide the technology teachers will somehow sense or automatically know how to use it. If I were to list the five biggest fallacies about technology in education, this would be near the top of the list. You can provide all the new technology in the world, but if teachers are not trained in how to use it, they will not use it. It is a strange commentary when school districts will provide the technology but not train educators to use it.

- Keep Up with New Ideas in Technology. This seems like such a basic idea to me that perhaps it does not need to be included, but it is important. For some reason education and school librarianship seem to be professions in which getting the degree or certification means turning off the "learning light" for many. This whole idea of keeping up with new ideas in technology can, in fact, be expanded to keeping up with new ideas in school librarianship. Very few school districts provide tangible rewards for those who keep up with new ideas, but it is certainly part of your professional responsibility to do so. We keep coming back to it, but failing to keep up with new ideas in either technology or librarianship is doing a disservice to your students. This is a tough requirement, but you have to make the time to at least keep up with technology innovations through your professional reading.

### Additional Technology Skills

The skills we have just discussed are key technology skills for the school librarian. There really is no room for negotiation: you must have these skills. Following are six other areas of technology skills that, while important, are not as key as the previous five.

1. Managing Library Technology Projects. One of the skills we all must use as school librarians is the ability to manage library technology projects. Ideas are wonderful when one implements technology, whether it is upgrading your OPAC or a major project like providing a computer, Internet access, and a work space to every user in your library. If you want to see these good ideas come to fruition, you had better be able to plan and manage the project because the reality is that if it is going to be done, it will be your responsibility. Plan carefully so that if your plan is approved you are ready to move right into the implementation phase. Be sure you have answers to questions that might be asked and also have alternative plans. There are several good planning models available. Select the one you like best and follow it.

2. Determine Why You Do Things in Your Library. This is a long title for a single word: Question. Why do you do what you do in your library? Too often we do things or set policies that do not benefit anyone but ourselves or we have policies that seem to be outmoded. This again relates not just to technology but to library policies as well. With relation to technology, one policy nearly every school library and even school district seems to have in force is forbidding the use of cell phones by students in school.

Many reasons are given for this prohibition. Cell phones can be disruptive. Cell phones can be used to cheat on examinations. Cell phones can be used to communicate with others surreptitiously. These are all true. However, by banning the use of cell phones, we are prohibiting a very powerful piece of new technology, one that not only has communication capabilities, but one that can be used to gather information. Blackberries and I Phones are not just telephones but sophisticated computing devices having good, cogent educational uses. Perhaps in light of this one might want to revisit a policy that bans cell phones completely.

3. Be Able to Determine Who Needs What. When you are planning for technology it is crucial to see which of your constituencies needs what. Consider what your students need, what your teachers need, what the school administration needs, and what the parents need. Also, and equally important, consider what the library staff needs. In this hierarchy of things, what you need generally falls last. When you consider the needs of these different constituent groups, the group that should be satisfied first is the students. We are in the business of educating and providing information to them. Ignore their needs at your peril!

One other constituent group's needs have to be considered and that is those of the library staff. You may have great ideas about technology, but if your staff is not on board, whatever technology plans you have will certainly fail.

4. Translate Traditional Library Services into an Online Medium. As we move forward into the twenty-first century, it is becoming evident that education is increasingly delivered to students in nontraditional ways with digital schools leading the way. Online education has been growing for the past twenty years, but until recently the focus has been on postsecondary education. As a matter of fact, a for-profit, primarily online institution, the University of Phoenix, is now the largest university in the United States.

This movement to online education is spreading into the K–12 education arena as well, with the spread of digital and cyber schools. Who are the students in these schools? It varies, but the typical cyber school students generally fall into three categories. First are students who are being homeschooled. Using cyber schools takes much of the burden off the parents of homeschoolers. Second are those students who for health or legal reasons are not able to attend traditional schools. The third category is those students who select only certain courses to take through the cyberschool. An example of this would be a student whose high school offers only a limited number of Advanced Placement or higher-level courses. They can attend the cyberschool to make up these needs.

It is incumbent on the school librarian, then, to provide a digital library to these students. The entire issue of digital libraries will be discussed in Chapter 8, but the tech-savvy school librarian must be able to convert traditional library services such as reference and instruction to an online medium. It is just not enough to provide online students access to the Internet; they must also have access to sophisticated library services.

5. Be Critical of Technology. This competency seems to be a dichotomy because we have emphasized so much the need to understand and use technology, and here we are saying to be critical of technology. Accepting all technology unquestioningly is as bad as not having any technology at all. A term Farkas (2009) uses is "technolust," which is wanting to have everything just because it is technology.

A school librarian has so many legitimate uses for technology that it is not really necessary to have every bit of new technology. Part of the task is to evaluate what is the best technology for a particular task and if, in fact, technology is needed at all. Technology is not a panacea for all of your needs in the school library. You must be critical of technology, both hardware and software, and be sure it can be integrated into the school library. Use of Web 2.0 social networking applications can really appeal to your students, but if you cannot integrate it into your library's program, you should not be using it.

While you may want all of the technology, if you are to maintain your credibility with your administration, you will have to be judicious in the technology you implement. Use technology to fill a need, not just because it is nice to have.

6. Be Able to Sell Technology in the Library. Few of us signed on to be school librarians in order to be salespeople, but it is such an essential part of the job that it cannot be overlooked. After you plan for the technology you want in your school library, you have to sell its value to your building and district administration. Many school districts have begun dividing budget requests into needs and wants categories. If your technology plans and requests fall into the wants instead of the needs category, the chances of being funded become less as budgets become tighter and tighter.

This is not all of the selling that has to be done, however. You must be able to sell your technology ideas to your faculty so they appreciate its usefulness and want to use it. You must be the cheerleader for your library program and be able to convince your faculty it is an integral part of the school. If you cannot, or if you will not, you will soon become superfluous.

# WHAT CAN LIBRARY SCHOOLS DO?

The answer to this is obvious: library schools must offer more courses that relate to technology in the school library. Simply offering courses in application software is not enough. Courses related to Web page design, telecommunications, and integrating traditional library services into technology would be a good starting place. Perhaps even more important is providing the school librarian with the skills and attitudes to adapt and change with technology. All types of technology will change as time goes by. If school librarians have the ability to adapt as technology changes they will be successful.

## Specific Technology Skills for School Librarians

Surprisingly little has been written about the technology skills that school librarians will need to be successful. It is again almost as though we, as school librarians, are expected to know about technology through osmosis, without any training at all. Following are two lists of technology skills needed by school librarians and a more detailed explanation of what is included in the skill. The first list is based on material prepared by the Colorado Department of Education in 1999 (Colorado 1999). The second group of competencies was prepared by a commercial concern in 2005 but remain relevant today. You will note there are many overlaps in the two lists but significant differences as well.

## Colorado Technology Skills

These skills, formulated more than ten years ago, are detailed and break the skills into four areas:

1. Basic Computer and Technology Operations and Concepts. These would be skills that provide school librarians with the basic ability to operate a computer and other technology tools. Included in this basic area would be the following:
   - Computer Operations
     - Assemble a computer system and be able to start up and shut down the computer and its peripherals.
     - Identify and use basic parts of the workspace, including icons, separate windows, and menus.

- Start an application and prepare output from that application.
- Use the operating system to name, save, find, retrieve, and revise output from applications
- Set up, add, delete, and use different types of printers.
- Use storage devices including hard drives, floppy disks, flash drives, CD-ROMs, and DVDs.
- Use the operating system to copy files among and between different storage mediums.
- Use the operating system to save, open, and put documents in subfolders and directories.
- Multitask; open and use more than one application at a time.
- Use more than one platform effectively. Ideally this would be several versions of Windows and Macintosh.
- Initialize and name and rename the storage devices described above.
- Create, name, and rename folders and subdirectories within your operating system.
- Run programs from networks or CDs and DVDs.
- Maintenance and Troubleshooting
  - Care for computer hardware and storage media.
  - Prepare backups of documents, files, and the system.
  - Keep printers supplied with paper, toner, and ink cartridges, as appropriate.
  - Perform first echelon maintenance on computers, peripheral devices, and local network connections.
  - Prepare and follow troubleshooting checklists and procedures for computers, peripheral devices, and networks.
  - Address environmental issues when planning areas for computers and peripherals in your library.
  - Protect your technology from computer viruses.
  - Know the steps to follow to obtain next level technical assistance.

2. Personal and Professional Use of Technology in the School Library. These are the skills that allow you to apply technology tools for productivity in the school library and for the school librarians' personal use. Included in this area would be the following:
   - Word Processing and Desktop Publishing
     - Create and edit text.
     - Use the cut, copy, and paste functions, including the extended capabilities.
     - Format and style documents, including fonts and font size, margins, line spacing, tabs, and bullets and numbering.

- Spell and grammar check documents.
- Create, edit, and copy headers and footers.
- Insert, edit, and move date, time, and page numbers in documents.
- Add columns to documents and manipulate section breaks to change column setup.
- Insert, populate, and edit tables in a document.
- Insert, edit, and change all types of graphics in a document.
- Create and change mail merges.
- Create and apply styles and templates.
- Import and insert data from other applications.
- Create PDF and HTML documents from word processing documents.
- Spreadsheets and Charting
  - Plan and interpret a spreadsheet.
  - Change or modify existing spreadsheets, including formatting and appearance.
  - Create a new spreadsheet with appropriate rows, columns, and headings.
  - Create and copy formulas to calculate within a spreadsheet.
  - Use functions within a spreadsheet to simplify formulas and calculation.
  - Understand and use correctly, relative, absolute, and mixed cell references.
  - Create appropriate charts from spreadsheet data.
  - Sort spreadsheet data.
  - Use spreadsheet data to create reports.
  - Create PDF and HTML documents from charts and spreadsheet data.
- Databases
  - Interpret and effectively communicate database information.
  - Add, delete, and modify records in a database.
  - Use specific fields to sort a database.
  - Extract data that meets specific criteria.
- Networks
  - Use local area networks to connect, log on and log off, open a program, retrieve a document, and save a document.
  - Use the network to share files with other users.
  - Understand network terminology including local area network (LAN), wide area network (WAN), access rights, security, passwords, file server, and zone.
- Telecommunications

- Use both local and network connections to connect to the Internet.
- Understand the difference among Internet search engines and use the appropriate search engine.
- Use different Web browsers and locate resources quickly and effectively.
- Download and print Web resources in different formats.
- Use the social networking features of the Web 2.0 including, blogs, wikis, podcasting, virtual conferencing, and virtual sites with avatars.
- Effectively locate data and information on the hidden Web.
- Manage bookmarks or their equivalent in all browsers.
- Access and use resources from appropriate states' databases for books and electronic data.
- Use e-mail tools including compose, send, retrieve, read, reply, forward, delete, and archive.
- Create e-mail accounts.
- Attach different types of files to e-mail.
- Retrieve and view, read, save, and print attachments in different formats.
- Create and use contacts and groups using the address book feature of e-mail.
- Use e-mail, Web sites, and other types of discussion media to collaborate with professional colleagues.
- Create Web sites and pages to be posted to the World Wide Web.
- Connect to the Internet using all types of connections and understand the limitations of each type of connection.
- Use Internet resources when not online.
- Install, configure, and use telecommunications software.
- Configure and use an FTP program to communicate with remote computer sites.
- Use technology for instructional purposes including distance learning and desktop video conferencing.
- Media Communications Use
  - Prepare and operate video media to include VCRs, DVD players, laser disk players, and streaming video.
  - Set up large-screen displays connected to computers and other video sources.
  - Use paint, draw, and authoring tools to enhance other electronic media.
  - Use multimedia presentation software to plan, create, and use both linear and nonlinear presentations.

- Use imaging devices such as digital cameras, video cameras, or scanners with computer systems and software.
- Produce and edit a videotape and then digitize it.
- Know when and how to use file compression utilities.
- Add digitized sound from audio sources to presentations.
- Apply animation techniques to presentations and Web pages.

3. Integrate Technology into the Curriculum. The technology skills at this level are becoming more sophisticated. This level moves us past simple technology skills to integration and synthesis of technology skills with curriculum planning. These are essential technology skills because the use of technology or teaching technology skills to students not in context lessens transfer learning and eliminates that tie to the curriculum. The technology skills included in this area would include the following:

- Curriculum
  - Create learning experiences for students that are appropriate to the curriculum, relevant to different learning styles, based on principles of effective learning and teaching, incorporate media and technology where appropriate, using a variety of media communication tools.
  - Use literacy instruction to guide students in accessing, synthesizing, and using information resources.
  - Consider students' technical skills when developing and using lesson plans.
  - Use the Internet and other telecommunications channels to gain access to educational resources for planning and instruction.
  - Use all technology resources to assist in locating, evaluating, and selecting appropriate teaching and learning resources and curriculum resources for content and target audiences.
- Design and Management of Learning Environments and Resources.
  - Develop tasks that will require students to locate, analyze, and draw conclusions about information and use a variety of media to communicate their findings.
  - Collect information about student learning using computers and other technology media appropriately and effectively.
  - Communicate a variety of information about student learning to colleagues, parents, and others using computers and other technology.
  - Recognize and create physical settings that support student involvement, inquiry, and collaboration.

- Create and implement organizational and management strategies that support student involvement, inquiry, and collaboration.
- Insure that all types of technology resources are available.
- Child Development, Learning, and Diversity
  - Address differences in children's learning, learning styles, and performance using media and technology.
  - Support learning for special needs children using media and technology.
  - Use a variety of media and technology to support learning for children whose primary language is not English.
  - Use all levels of services or resources, local, state, or national, to meet a variety of learning needs through technology.
  - Modify computers and input and output devices to enable all students, regardless of disabilities, to create, manipulate, store, and distribute information.
- Social, Legal, and Ethical Issues
  - Know and enforce school district policies and procedures and federal law concerning copyright law and fair-use guidelines.
  - Be responsible, ethical, and legal when using technical information and software resources.
  - Provide equal access to media and technology resources regardless of students' race, ethnicity, gender, religion, or socioeconomic status.

4. Building Level Technical Support. These skills may seem strange to see on a list of technology skills a school librarian should possess, but as we have discussed earlier, a general low level of technology staffing in public schools makes many of these skills necessary for the efficient use of technology. You cannot just put an out-of-order sign on technology that is not working and wait for someone to come and fix it. Pretty soon you will have all signs and no technology. Among the required skills are the following:

- Setting up computer systems and correctly attaching peripheral devices.
- Cleaning computer components and printers. Keep a big supply of canned air and alcohol wipes on hand.
- Install, reinstall, and update system software and printer drivers.
- Make memory available by manipulating system software.
- Diagnose and correct common basic hardware and printing problems using self-help resources.
- Understand and troubleshoot basic computer setup configurations.
- Add users and assign passwords on the network server.

- Maintain the local area network (LAN).
- Install, reinstall, and update application software.
- Understand the design and configuration of your local area network.

This is certainly a daunting list, but the fact remains that if you are to be a technologically able school librarian, these are really a minimum set of required skills. Each one of the categories enumerated could have many, many more skills added and still just scratch the surface of what is required. One of the charges I received from the Chair of the Department of Education at St. Vincent College when I began teaching a course in technology for prospective school librarians was to teach them everything they need to know about technology. My rejoinder was that I would probably not live long enough to do that but that I would do my best.

Listed below is perhaps a simpler list of skills required of educators. This is a current (2005) list based on research done by Skytech Dynamics Corporation, and while the skills have been reduced to twenty, they are still inclusive. The skills are broken into twenty categories and then include a bit more about each one. It could become your list of staff development programs to offer your teachers.

1.  Word Processing. Educators should be able to use some type of word processing program to complete written tasks in a timely manner. While Microsoft Word is most widely used, you should be knowledgeable with two or three other word processing programs in common use.

2.  Spreadsheets. Educators should be able to use some type of spreadsheet program to compile grades and chart data. Again, Microsoft Excel is pretty standard. For school librarians there are many other spreadsheet applications, such as budgeting, that are valuable.

3.  Databases. Educators should be able to use some type of database program to create tables, store and retrieve data, and query data. Microsoft Access is a full relational database. It has more power than most school librarians would need but is still a very valuable application.

4.  Electronic Presentations. Educators should be able to use electronic presentation software to create and give electronic presentations. Microsoft PowerPoint is pretty much the industry standard. School librarians need to be aware of both the linear and nonlinear capabilities of electronic presentation software.

5.  World Wide Web Navigation. Educators should be able to navigate and search the World Wide Web for data on the Internet. There are a wide variety of Internet search engines available

that often return different results for the same search term. Your students will be locked into Google; expand their horizons with other search engines. Do not forget to use metasearch engines such as Dogpile.

6. Web Site Design. Educators should be able to design, create, and maintain a faculty/educator Web page/site. It is incumbent on school librarians to create a Web presence for their library that is available both in school and at home. This skill requires some specialized training and a relationship with the school district's technology coordinator or Web master.

7. E-mail Management. Educators should be able to use e-mail to communicate and be able to send attachments and create e-mail folders. This is really the technology skill that will make or break you as a technology expert with your faculty. They will come to you with questions about e-mail, and if the perception is that you do not know, you will have lost a golden opportunity.

8. Digital Cameras. Educators should be able to operate a digital camera and understand how digital imaging can be used. This is an easy one and one that you can use to show off your expertise. Always have your digital camera with you when you are having events in your library and post those pictures to your Web site!

9. Network Knowledge. Educators should know the basics of computer networks and understand how their school network works. This is a skill that you should have some basic knowledge of, but in-depth technical expertise is not required unless you are also the technology coordinator. You do need to know the difference between real network issues and an unplugged network connection.

10. File Management and Windows Explorer. Educators should be able to manage their computer files including: create and delete files and folders, move and copy files and folders, and use Windows Explorer. One statement is applicable here: "I know I saved that file but now I can't find it."

11. Downloading Software from the Web (this includes e-Books). Educators should be able to download software from the Web and be aware of sites that can be used for that purpose. As a corollary to this, school librarians need to be aware of the legal and ethical issues that are involved with downloading software.

12. Installing Computer Software onto a Computer System. Educators should be able to install computer software onto a computer system. You should be able to install on both a stand-alone computer and onto your school's computer network. Some knowledge of creating software models and ghosting is also important.

13. Online Learning Systems. Educators should be aware of the leading online learning systems and know about them and how to use them to teach or take online classes. These are essential skills that have come to the fore in the past few years. Online education is now available and accredited at all levels. This relates closely to digital libraries.

14. Video Conferencing. Educators should be able to use a video conferencing classroom and know the basics of teaching with video conferencing. The equipment involved with video conferencing is quite expensive, but there are generally grants available for the purchase of the equipment. Quite often the video conferencing equipment is maintained in the school library and the school librarian is responsible for its use.

15. Computer-Related Storage Devices. Educators should understand and know how to use data storage devices including, hard disks, floppy disks, CDs, USB drives, and DVDs. This is one of the most rapidly changing areas of technology. Floppy disks are rarely used today, and the new technology appears to be storage on remote servers even for home computer users.

16. Scanners. Educators should know how to use a scanner and know what Optical Character Recognition (OCR) software is and how to use OCR software. Scanner skills are particularly important when working with digitization projects. Knowing how to use OCR software is important, but school librarians need to be aware of its shortcomings.

17. Personal Digital Assistants (PDAs). Educators should know what a PDA is and how to use one. This is a must for the technologically savvy school librarian. Whether it is a Palm, a Blackberry, or some other PDA, you had better be using one, and not a paper appointment book.

18. Deep Web (also known as the Hidden Web). Educators should know what the Deep Web is and how to use it as a resource. This is a much-overlooked area of the Web that has excellent statistical data. If your students think Google gives them all that they need on the Web, guide them to the Deep Web.

19. Educational Copyright. Educators should understand the copyright issues that relate to education, including multimedia and Web-based copyright issues. Far, far too many teachers use the approach that because they are using things for education they can ignore copyright law. This is far from true.

20. Computer Security. Educators should know about basic computer security issues related to education. As a school librarian you

need to have a wide range of knowledge in this area. Even though you probably will not be able to actually implement many of the security procedures yourself, you need to know about them. Just remember that your technology coordinator does not want to allow access through the firewall!

## CLOSING THOUGHTS

After introducing school libraries without technology and the importance of technology to the school librarian, we have moved in this chapter to a detailed examination of the technology skills that are required for the school librarian to be a vital and viable force. We have moved from a theoretical look at technology skills to an extremely practical pair of lists of important technology skills for the school librarian. This sets the stage for forthcoming chapters that will examine in detail all issues related to technology and the school librarian.

The technology skills a school librarian must possess are mind-boggling. Many will say "I don't need these," but the reality is that the school librarian needs these skills desperately—they are not negotiable if one is to be relevant in education and keep their job. These skills should be part of the package any twenty-first-century school librarian should have in their repertoire. Without them the school librarian is just a purveyor of books. Chapter 3 will examine in detail technology hardware and computer software for school libraries. Of note is the discussion of the "ideal" student computer.

## RESOURCES

American Library Association. "AASL Information Power Action Research Project." AASL. http://www.ala.org/ala/mgrps/divs/aasl/aaslproftools/informationpower/informationpower.cfm (accessed January 11, 2009).

Burke, John J. *Neal-Schuman Library Technology Companion: A Basic Guide for Library Staff.* New York: Neal-Schuman, 2004.

Coish, David. (2005). Canadian School Libraries and Teacher-Librarians: Results from the 2003–2004 Information and Communications Technologies in Schools Survey. http://www.statcan.gc.ca/pub/81-004-x/2005002/8051-eng.htm (accessed January 25, 2009).

"Colorado Technology Competency Guidelines for Classroom Teachers and School Library Media Specialists." http://www.eric.ed.gov/ERICWebPortal/custom/portlets/recordDetails/detailmini.jsp?_nfpb=true&_&ERICExtSearch_SearchValue_0=ED433020&ERICExtSearch_SearchType_0=no&accno=ED433020 (accessed January 14, 2009).

Credaro, A. B. "Skill Sets for School Librarians." Warrior Librarian Weekly. http://warriorlibrarian.com/FOUND/skillset.html (accessed January 14, 2009).

Doggett, Sandra L. *Beyond the Book: Technology Integration into the Secondary School Library Media Curriculum*. Englewood: Libraries Unlimited, 2000.

Eisenberg, Michael, and Doug Johnson. "Learning and Teaching Information Technology Computer Skills in Context." http://www.libraryinstruction.com/info-tech.html (accessed January 14, 2009).

Farkas, Meredith. "Skills for the 21st Century Librarian." http://meredith.wolfwater.com/wordpress/2006/07/17/skills-for-the-21st-century-librarian/ (accessed January 14, 2009).

Hartzell, Gary N. "The Invisible School Librarian: Why Other Educators Are Blind to Your Value." *School Library Journal*, Nov. 1997. http://www.schoollibraryjournal.com/index.asp?layout=articleArchive&articleid=CA152978 (accessed February 3, 2009).

Jurkowski, Odin L. *Technology and the School Library: A Comprehensive Guide for Media Specialists and Other Educators*. Lanham, MD: Scarecrow, 2006.

Kochtanek, Thomas R., and Joseph R. Matthews. *Library Information Systems: From Library Automation to Distributed Information Access Solutions*. Westport, CT: Libraries Unlimited, 2002.

Kohn, John M., Ann L. Kelsey, and Keith Michael Fields. *Planning for Integrated Systems and Technologies: A How-To-Do-It Manual for Librarians*. New York: Neal-Schuman, 2001.

Lowe, Carrie. "The Role of the School Library Media Specialist in the 21st Century." Eric Digest. http://www.ericdigests.org/2001-3/21st.htm (accessed January 14, 2009).

NCLIS. (2008). "School Libraries Work." http://www2.scholastic.com/content/collateral_resources/pdf/s/slw3_2008.pdf (accessed January 14, 2009).

"School Libraries—An Under-Resourced Resource?" http://www.statcan.gc.ca/pub/81-004-x/2005002/8051-eng.htm (accessed January 14, 2009).

Turner, Laura. "20 Technology Skills Every Educator Should Have." http://www.instructor.aviation.ca/content/view/133/71 (accessed January 14, 2009).

Williams, Brad. *We're Getting Wired, We're Going Mobile, What's Next? Fresh Ideas for Educational Technology Planning*. Eugene, OR: ISTE, 2004.

# QUESTIONS FOR RESEARCH AND DISCUSSION

1. The lists of technology skills and competencies for educators and school librarians are necessarily dated as of the writing of this book. In order to bring these lists up to date, research the topic "Technology Skills for School Librarians." Compare what you found with the lists included in this chapter and discuss any changes or additions you found. Be sure to comment on items or skills that are no longer considered crucial.

2. Based on your reading of this chapter and your research, prepare your detailed list of important technology skills for school librarians. Share your list with your classmates and revise your list. You should include detailed discussion as to why the skills you selected are important. Then take your revised list to both your technology coordinator and your principal for comment. Summarize their comments and add them to your list.

3. Lack of preparation of prospective school librarians in the school library certification programs is listed as a factor in their not being effective users and purveyors of technology. Research the requirements at three institutions and determine the level of coursework in technology required of preservice school librarians. Your task is to prepare a model course(s) that would adequately prepare school librarians to effectively use technology. Be sure to justify your choices and include the educational outcomes for the course(s).

4. You have just been appointed the library department chair for the Anytown School District and find there has never been any technology training provided to the school librarians. Your task is to prepare a three-year technology training plan for the school librarians. Your plan should be based on your readings and research and be in sufficient detail that it could be implemented immediately.

# 3

# *Networks, Hardware, and Software for School Libraries*

In Chapter 2 we discussed the technology skills that all school librarians should possess. In this chapter we will discuss networks, hardware, and software that school librarians should have knowledge of if they are to be technology leaders in their schools. Certainly not all schools will have all of these things, and not all school librarians will work with all of these aspects of networking, all of the hardware devices, or all of the types of software. In point of fact this chapter should represent an introduction to these things for school librarians. An outline of networking concepts and terminology is provided, along with a discussion of different types of computer hardware and computer software. The aim is to provide the school librarian with some base of knowledge upon which they can build as different aspects of technology enter their libraries.

It was mentioned in Chapter 1 that most school libraries are at a particular level of technology acceptance: the bleeding edge, the leading edge, in the wedge, or in the trailing edge. No matter the level of technology acceptance, it is essential that school librarians be able to intelligently evaluate technology choices before they are purchased. Several criteria are available, but the one part put forth by Matthews (2004, 4–7) is quite appropriate. When evaluating technology choices one should consider the following:

- Is it suitable? In other words, does it meet the need for which it is designed. This is an area that those on the bleeding edge often ignore.
- Is the technology nearing obsolescence? This is a hard area for school librarians to judge, but they should not hesitate to ask if something newer is close to introduction. What makes this a difficult issue is how obsolete will the technology become. As an example, Windows Vista has been available for more than three years, but the previous operating system, Windows XP, is still used in many schools.

- How durable is the technology? For school librarians this is almost a no-brainer. The technology purchased for schools must withstand the wear, tear, and rough use that kids will give it. If it cannot, do not buy it.
- Does the technology fit in the library environment? It is incumbent on the school librarian to determine if the technology really fits the needs of their library and also if the technology works in the physical footprint of the school library.
- Are there training implications for the technology? You have to determine if the learning curve for technology is high or low. Pieces of hardware and software that are not intuitive and have steep learning curves will be difficult for you to learn and perhaps impossible to teach to your teachers. Those types of technology might not be appropriate for all school library situations.
- Does the technology have maintenance, updating, or upgrading requirements? Almost all technology today does, but you must determine if it is so onerous as to make it a major issue. Determine if these things are easy to do or if they require outside intervention. Are maintenance arguments available?
- Is there support available if there are problems with the technology? This is closely related to the previous point. No one wants to spend extended periods on the telephone with a help center. Help must be affordable and easily obtainable.
- Is the technology cost effective? In these days of decreasing school library budgets, this is an essential element. Are there other technologies that do almost the same thing for less money or is the technology absolutely unique?
- Is the technology the most appropriate way to provide the service? This is where the rubber meets the road for the school librarian. Just because there is technology available to accomplish a particular task does not mean that is the best way to do things. The truth is that sometimes a pen and paper is the best, most cost-effective technology to accomplish a task.

## NETWORKS

### *What Is a Network?*

As the use of computers has grown in school libraries, so too has the use of networked computers. In the early days of personal computers, they were typically stand-alone. This means all applications were contained on each computer and information could only be shared by using storage devices such as floppy disks. Most home computers are still stand-alone machines because of the cost and technical skills required to have a network in the home.

As time passed it became more and more necessary for computers to be networked. Stand-alone machines just did not meet the requirements of computing and technology in the school library. In simplest terms a network is a group of connected computers. Expanding this definition a bit, a network is a group of connected computers that can exchange information with each other.

### Home Networks

Most networks can be defined as home networks, local area networks (LAN), or wide area networks (WAN). Home networks are just what the name implies, a network within one's home. A home network may be either a wired network or a wireless network, and while data sharing may be a goal of a home network, it is most often used as a single path to the Internet. With a home network each computer can work through a router and single modem to connect to the Internet.

### Local Area Networks

A local area network (LAN) is a computer network that serves or covers a small geographical area. Based on this definition a home network could be a LAN, but more typically a LAN covers a building or group of buildings such as a school, campus, or an office. In contrast to wide area networks (a WAN), a LAN is usually characterized by higher data transmission rates, smaller physical areas covered, and not having a need for leased or purchased tele-communication lines. As noted earlier, the use of a network allows users to share data and information, but there are some very cogent reasons why a LAN is to be favored over stand-alone computers in a school library:

- Fewer peripheral devices are needed because that can be shared by LAN users. No longer does each computer have to have its own printer.
- All types of information can be shared.
- Software programs can be shared.
- Users have access to resources when needed, minimizing downtime.
- If devices on the network are not functioning they can be bypassed and other devices used.
- Telecommunication costs can be minimized.
- Licensed databases can be shared within the school library.

- Moving and sharing data is accomplished electronically rather than physically.
- Resources can be added incrementally.

While you as the school librarian will probably not get involved in the wiring of a building LAN unless you are also the technology coordinator, you need to be aware of the components of the LAN, including the wiring, the network topology, the access method, and the network design, so that you can talk with the persons doing the installation. The type of wiring used in the construction of the LAN determines the bandwidth and the data rate of the network. In prior years these were considerations most related to cost, but as sound and video have become much more common, the size of the pipeline and how fast data can be moved have taken on an even more important aspect. Three general types of communications media are available: twisted-pair cable, coaxial cable, and fiber optic cable.

The cheapest is twisted-pair cable. This has a data rate of 10 Mbps (megabits per second) and a bandwidth of 500 KHz. Twisted-pair cable has typically been used for telephone voice communications and for data transmission. Of the three communications media, twisted-pair is the cheapest and easiest to work with, but is also has the smallest capacity and is the slowest.

Coaxial cable is the second type of communications media. Its data rate is 500 Mbps and its bandwidth is 550 KHz. Often coaxial cable, which is most commonly used for television cable, will be the backbone of a LAN, with twisted-pair cable branching from the backbone cable. Coaxial cable is less vulnerable to interference and has much more bandwidth than twisted-pair cable.

By far the fastest is fiber optic cable. Along with this much greater capability is an extremely high cost. For school districts the high cost of fiber makes it impractical for purchase, but recently consortiums have negotiated group prices for fiber, bringing it within the budget of school districts.

### Wide Area Networks

A WAN is one that covers a wider geographic area than does a local area network. A couple of examples should help to clarify this point. The city of Philadelphia has a wireless network that allows all of its residents to connect to the Internet. While this is technically a metropolitan area network (MAN), it is also an example of a WAN. While some might consider a network that connects all the facilities of a school district as still being a local area network, for our purposes it would be considered a WAN because it allows the local area network in each school facility to be connected. The largest and by far best-known wide area network is the Internet.

Many WANs are proprietary and are for use by a particular entity. Typically these types of networks require authentication in order to enter the network. Other wide area networks are constructed by Internet service providers like Comcast or Verizon and are used to provide connections from individual computers or local area networks to the Internet.

### *LANs versus WANs in the School Library*

If the school library has its own LAN, all library-related software is housed on the library's server and the library does not share any tasks or even records with other school libraries in the district. In other words, each school library has its own local area network that does not connect to other school libraries. On the other hand, in a WAN environment library software is stored on a network server in a central location and all of the school libraries share their resources. While the latter is the overwhelming environment used by most school districts, there are some advantages and disadvantages of each.

### Local Area-Based Configurations

| Advantages | Disadvantages |
| --- | --- |
| 1. Faster access to the collection because access is local | 1. A limited collection is available because only local holdings are seen |
| 2. Easier and faster diagnosis of problems and hardware troubleshooting | 2. Local control over the database |
| 3. If a Web server is maintained the school library's OPAC can be available on the Web | |
| 4. Only local holdings are visible (many would also consider this a disadvantage) | |

### Wide Area Configurations

| Advantages | Disadvantages |
| --- | --- |
| 1. Access the holdings of multiple school libraries | 1. Access may be slower because of high traffic levels |
| 2. Consistency through centralized cataloging | 2. Server malfunctions will affect the entire system, not just one school library |
| 3. Wide Area network software more economical than local area network software | 3. High learning curve |

# NETWORK TOPOLOGY

Just as your school library has a floor plan that was developed to allow the most efficient use of resources and facilities, networks have different blueprints for their layouts. Network topology refers to the physical arrangement of computers, cabling, and other network components. The three most common network topologies are bus, ring, and star. The type of topology used for a network helps determine the network's performance. Just as one plan may not be satisfactory for all school libraries, not all network topologies are equally efficient.

### Bus Topology

In a bus topology network, all computers and peripherals are connected in sequence as shown in the figure below. The bus topology is most often used on a peer-to-peer (P2P) network and rarely on a client-server network. In the bus topology network each computer can communicate with every other computer. Advantages of bus topology networks are their simple design and low cost. Furthermore, no server is required. There are several disadvantages of this topology, many of which mitigate against the proliferation and growth of bus topology networks. First, if there is a break in the cable the computers are cut off from one another and the network is effectively disabled. Second, as the distance of the cabling and number of nodes on the network increases, performance is degraded. Early AppleTalk networks used the bus topology.

### Ring Topology

In a ring topology, often called loop topology, the nodes on the ring, computers and/or peripherals, are in a configuration that looks like a circle as shown in Figure 1. Data flow around this circle and are passed from computer to computer until they reach the computer for which they are intended. Ring topologies are sometimes called token ring networks because the data are transmitted using a special data packet called a token. The primary advantage of the ring topology is that even with large numbers of nodes the performance is at an acceptable level. Like the bus, the ring topology network is stopped if one computer in the ring fails. Furthermore, problems on a ring can be hard to find or diagnose.

### Star Topology

The star topology is the most widely used client/server network topology today. This topology is called a star because the network nodes connect to a central communications device called a switch as shown in Figure 1. You have probably heard of the Ethernet communications protocol that is used by many star networks. This communications protocol is a set of rules for the exchange of

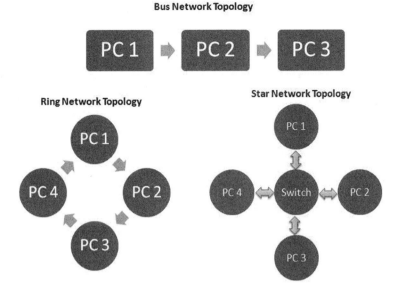

**Figure 1**　Network Topologies

communication. A star network has several advantages. First, if one computer fails, the performance of the network is not affected. Second, the addition of nodes to a star network typically does not degrade network performance, and third, the diagnosis of network problems is easier. The major disadvantages of a star network are the complexity of the cabling and the relatively high cost.

This description of different network topologies leads to one question; what is the best network topology? As networks have evolved over the years, it has become obvious that the star topology is the network design to use in school libraries. While they can be relatively pricey, the versatility and flexibility makes the star the network of choice. Just as you will rarely find a peer-to-peer network outside the home environment, the same is true for any network topology other than a star.

# NETWORKING BASICS

## *Network Architecture*

A network's architecture refers to how a network is designed, how networks are controlled, and the distance between network nodes. When you hear people discuss how a network is administered or controlled, it refers to either local control or central control. A peer-to-peer network is the most common type of a locally administered network, while a client/server network is the most commonly encountered type of centrally administered network. While peer-to-peer networks are the most common type of home network and may even be effectively used in a small school, most networks with ten or more nodes are client/server networks.

A client/server network is comprised of two types of computers, clients and servers. The client is the computer that users use to complete tasks. The server is the computer that provides information or resources to the clients on the network. The server also provides the control, or central administration for the network. In addition to being a wide area network, the Internet is a type of client/server network. When connected to the Internet, your own computer is a client and your Internet service provider (ISP) is the service that allows you to access the Internet.

### Network Components

In order to operate, all networks must have a way for the nodes to connect to the network. This may be either cable or wireless. Furthermore, devices that allow the nodes to communicate and send data and software that control the network's operation are required.

### Transmission Media

All of the nodes of a network, both computers and peripherals, connect to each other and to the network using a transmission media, such as existing wiring, additional cabling, or wireless technology. The additional cabling used to connect network nodes can be twisted-pair cable, coaxial cable, or fiber optic cable. These cabling options were discussed earlier in this chapter. Wireless networks use radio waves to connect network nodes rather than wiring or cable.

The different types of transmission media transmit data through networks at different speeds. The bandwidth, which is also called the data transfer rate, measures the maximum speed data can be sent between two nodes. The throughput is the actual speed of data transfer and is generally slower than the data transfer rate. The bandwidth and the throughput are measured in megabits per second (Mbps), which represents 1 million bits.

### Network Adapters

Devices installed in or connected to network nodes that allow the nodes to communicate with each other or get to the network are called network adapters. They may be external devices but are much more likely to be installed in the nodes and are known as network interface cards (NICs).

### Network Navigation

Data sent over transmission media in a network is often bundled and called packets. Network navigation devices such as routers and switches facilitate this data flow. Routers are navigation devices that transfer packets of data between two or more networks. This is the process that allows data to be transferred from the Internet to a computer. Switches are like traffic lights on a network. They receive the packets of data and direct them to the correct nodes on the same network.

### Networking Software

All client/server networks are controlled by specialized network operating software (NOS) such as Windows Server 2008 or SUSE Linux Enterprise. NOS handles requests for data, access to the Internet, and the use of peripherals for the entire network.

## CONNECTING TO THE INTERNET

It is estimated that over 350 million people around the world are connected to the Internet. The truth is that if you are not providing your students and staff with Internet access in your library, you are overlooking a service that is expected in today's school library. When we began experimenting with the Internet nearly fifteen years ago, the connection was a dial-up connection using a modem and standard telephone lines. As time passed, broadband connections became the best way to connect to the Internet and the preferred Internet connection method in school libraries. Broadband Internet connections include cable, satellite, and digital subscriber line (DSL).

### Dial-Up Connections

Although rapidly being replaced by broadband Internet connection, dial-up connections are still in use. All that is required to connect to the Internet is a telephone line that connects to an ISP and a dial-up modem in or attached to the computer. Due to the proliferation of broadband connections, new computers no longer have built-in modems; these have been replaced with networks interface cards.

At one time we could say that a dial-up connection was enough for the casual Internet user. That is no longer true as the casual user is more interested in downloading music and video, two things a dial-up connection does not support. This is the main disadvantage of a dial-up connection; it is too slow to do the things with the Internet that your students and staff will want to do.

### Broadband Connections

Broadband Internet connections are the connections of choice today for your library. As mentioned earlier, there are several types of broadband connections, but not all are available in all geographic locations. Furthermore, not all of these broadband services are necessarily available to school districts. At any rate, if your school district has not moved forward to a broadband Internet connection, it needs to do so as soon as possible.

The first broadband connection to the Internet is a Cable TV connection. The connection to the Internet is made with a standard coaxial cable. In order to use a cable connection you will have to have a cable modem and a network interface card. Although a cable connection is faster than a dial-up connection, there can be speed degradation during peak usage times.

A DSL, or digital subscriber line, connection to the Internet uses a dedicated telephone line to connect to the Internet. If you are using a DSL connection, you must have a DSL modem that connects the computer to the DSL line. One of the primary strengths of a DSL connection is that it is not affected by busy times and numerous users sharing the same line. The main drawback of a DSL connection is that you must be in relative proximity to the phone company central offices, because the signal seriously degrades past 18,000 feet (a little over three miles).

Fiber optic Internet connections use fiber optic cable to receive the Internet data. This connection is also called FiOS. The primary advantage of a FiOS connection is its very high speed. That speed, however, comes with a substantial financial cost. Furthermore, fiber optic cable is so costly to install it is only available in limited areas of the country.

Schools that do not have other high-speed Internet options may elect to access the Internet via satellite. Schools need a satellite dish and cable to connect the dish to their network. While speed is relatively high, the signal from the satellite to the disk can be affected by interference or adverse weather conditions. The use of satellite can also be affected by mountains and other physical obstacles such as tall buildings.

We previously discussed the use of wireless networks to transmit data. Similarly, a school district can use a combination of a broadband Internet connection and a wireless network to access the Internet. In this situation, the district must have line-of-sight connections with the facility where the Internet signal is received. That data is then transmitted wirelessly to the various facilities within the school district. This is becoming the Internet connection of choice for many school districts but it does present significant security issues.

## FAT AND THIN CLIENTS

When you are deciding what types of computers to place on your network, you may want to decide if thin clients would be appropriate. A thin client is not a full-service computer but rather almost a terminal accessing a server for nearly all software requirements. In contrast, a fat client is a full-service computer, even though it may still be attached to a network. Libraries are prime candidates for the use of thin clients because library users very often do not need all the power of a full-service computer. Furthermore, a significant cost savings can be realized if thin clients are used. Some advantages to consider when evaluating thin or fat clients include:

| Advantages: Thin Clients | Advantages: Fat Clients |
|---|---|
| 1. Lower IT costs because thin clients are managed through the server. | 1. Fewer server requirements. |
| 2. Thin clients are easier to secure because data generally does not reside on them. | 2. Better multimedia performance. |
| 3. Better data security again because the data resides on the server, not the thin client. | 3. More flexibility. |
| 4. Lower hardware costs because thin clients do not have a disk, application memory, or a powerful processor. | 4. Better peripheral support. |
| 5. Lower energy consumption. | |
| 6. Easier failure management as a thin client is generally just swapped out if it fails. | |
| 7. Less value to thieves. | |
| 8. Operable in dusty and dirty environments because they have far fewer moving parts. | |
| 9. Less network bandwidth required. | |
| 10. Simple hardware upgrades. Often obsolete full-service computers can be used as replacements for thin clients. | |
| 11. Lower noise levels. | |
| 12. Less wasted hardware. | |

These are issues that school libraries must consider if they are thinking about using thin clients on a network rather than full-service computers. The thing that makes thin clients the most attractive is the cost savings. You can get a lot of bang for your buck using thin clients but cost economics are sometimes outweighed by other factors.

## COMPUTER HARDWARE

The next items to consider are computer hardware. This category includes the computer itself and what is inside the computer box and peripherals such as storage devices, monitors, mice, sound devices, printers, and scanners. This is not an all-inclusive list because new items, considered computer hardware, are developed almost daily. As a corollary to the development of new hardware there is the seemingly geometric increase in computing power.

The cofounder of Intel, one of the large chip manufactures, Gordon Moore, posited a trend in computing hardware in 1958 that has held true for more than fifty years. He stated that the number of transistors inside the CPU (central processing unit) of a computer would increase so fast that CPU capacity and therefore computing capacity would double every 18 months

(Kochtanek 2002, 50). The performance of the computer industry since Moore published his findings has borne this out to the extent that his conclusions are now known as Moore's Law. What are the real implications of Moore's Law for school districts and school libraries? It means that unless you or your district has an unlimited supply of money, you will not always have the newest, best, and most powerful computers. Hard decisions will have to be made about when to purchase an upgrade, what to purchase or upgrade, and whether to purchase or lease the computer hardware.

In an ideal world we would be able to add new technology as it becomes available, but we know the ideal world does not exist. The school librarian can consider some options when purchasing computer hardware. First, always try the technology before you commit to buying or leasing it. Sometimes this may require a trip to a library with the technology you are considering, but it will be a trip that will pay for itself if you find what you are looking for. Second, always compare models and technologies. While you may not want hardware at the bleeding edge, neither do you want hardware that is inadequate for your needs or soon to become obsolete. Third, know the point when you have to stop looking and start buying. Sometimes we get too tied up in comparing and analyzing the options we cannot actually pull the trigger and buy. This is known as "paralysis by analysis." Finally, do not get caught in the trap of being influenced by any of the computer myths. Many myths are out there, including the myth that you should wait to purchase because the computer prices will stabilize. This has not happened for 50 years, why would it happen now? Another myth is you should wait to purchase because the prices will drop. There may be some truth to this myth, but it is reminiscent of a person who is known as a great shot. The problem is he never takes a shot because he is always waiting for the perfect shot. If you keep waiting for that price to drop just a bit more you will never purchase anything. The third myth is that delaying purchasing will allow current technology to become obsolete and new technology will be available. The question here is how long can you wait? Finally, you should never fall for the myth that just because technology is available and here it can be used. That is how schools end up with closets full of technology that is never used.

### Types of Computers

As was described in Chapter 1, the computer has evolved from a massive tube-operated machine with a very limited computing capacity to the handheld computing device such as a personal digital assistant (PDA). For the purpose of our discussion, we will consider three basic types of computers. First is the super computer. Only a few super computers are available in the world and they are used to perform very complex calculations very rapidly.

They are typically used when very intense mathematical calculations are required. Super computers are often shared by two or more universities. In geographic areas where there are super computers, their excess capability is often offered to students, but seldom to students in basic education.

The second basic type of computer is called a mainframe computer and is designed to support a large number of computer users at the same time. A mainframe computer is able to execute many different computer programs at the same time. Depending on its capacity it may also be called a mini-computer. School districts have moved forward to the point that many of them now own or lease mainframe computers. They are typically used for business applications in the school district or to host the school district's school management software. The school district's mainframe computer is often part of a school district network, so that functions such as building student schedules and grade book applications can be linked to the school district management software.

The third basic type of computer is the ubiquitous microcomputer. It comes in many brands and has many levels of capability, but it remains the computing backbone in school districts and school libraries. While the purpose of this book is not to champion one computer over another, there is an interesting phenomenon relating to Apple computers and Windows-based computers. In the early days of computing, schools were the province of Apple, while business was in the DOS- or Windows-based corner. At some point Apple made a business decision to try to move into the business arena. They were not successful in this attempt and at the same time appeared to forget their primary market was education. This failure to penetrate the business market also cost Apple their primacy in education. Now the Apple is a niche machine in a Windows world.

### Inside the Computer

Simply put, a computer is a data processing device with four functions: (1) It gathers data; (2) it processes data into information; (3) it outputs data or information; and (4) it stores data or information. Let us look at what is in the computer case, be it a desktop or notebook computer. The main thing that is in the computer case is the central processing unit or CPU. This is really what makes the computer compute. The CPU performs calculations and is responsible for processing input data into information. The CPU is located on the motherboard, the main circuit board in a computer. A number of different processors are available and include Pentium Dual Core, Centrino, and AMD processors. As a school librarian it is not always necessary to know all the technical specifics of the CPU, but there is a big question you should be prepared to answer: how fast should the CPU be in the computers you use? The simple answer, and perhaps it is an oversimplification, is that the CPU should be fast enough to meet the requirements of the hardware and software you use. What often happens is that as you add new components to the system the requirements on the CPU increase. Sooner or later your system will not support the new components and you will have to upgrade.

In addition to the CPU and motherboard, the computer case contains different circuit boards that perform functions for the computer. They generally are able to connect to other devices and are called expansion cards. Typical expansion cards might include sound cards, video cards, modem cards, and network interface cards. The computer case also contains the power supply for the computer and the memory modules, also called random access memory (RAM). RAM is the storage space for data and commands used by the CPU. There is a saying in technology that you can never have too much memory. The more memory your computer system has, the faster and more powerful it will be. The case of a computer will also contain a hard disk drive. While a hard drive is in fact a storage device, it is considered here because it is physically located in the computer case. It is the most efficient and fastest type of storage available and usually holds the system software, application software, as well as data and information. This brings us back to the question posed with reference to RAM: how big a hard drive is appropriate? Again technology experts would say you can never have too big a hard drive. The bigger the hard drive the more applications and data you can store.

### Computer Peripherals

Computer peripherals can be divided into two categories: input devices and output devices. Input devices include keyboards, mice, digital cameras, camcorders, webcams, and microphones. Specialized input devices are available to be used by physically challenged individuals. Output devices include monitors, printers, and speakers. In addition to input and output devices listed above, computer peripherals also include storage devices and scanners.

### Storage Devices

Several different types of storage devices can be used with computer systems. We mentioned hard drives contained in the computer case, but external hard drives are becoming more common as their price decreases. The advantage of an external hard drive is the speed at which it can be accessed and the high storage capacity. External hard drives connect to the computer through a universal serial bus (USB) port.

In the early days, the only real practical storage device was the floppy disk. In the earliest computers they were truly "floppy," but as the computer evolved, floppy disks standardized on 3.5 inch plastic disks. Today, very rarely do computers have floppy disk drives. The capacity of these early storage devices is just not large enough to hold meaningful amounts of information, and computers with floppy disk drives often have to be specially ordered. Similar to the floppy disk is the zip disk. A zip disk storage system has a higher storage capacity than a floppy disk, but the special zip disk requirements and the cost of the zip disks themselves hindered the widespread adoption of the zip disk system.

In most popular kinds of storage devices today are flash memory cards, flash drives, CD-ROMs, and DVDs. For day-to-day use, flash memory cards and flash drives are the most common. Flash memory cards are most often used with digital cameras, although information from flash memory cards is easily downloaded to computer systems. Flash drives are the most common type of mass storage used. The price of flash drives is dropping rapidly and the capacity is increasing rapidly. Flash drives connect to computer systems through USB ports.

CD-ROMs and DVDs are examples of optical storage devices that use lasers to etch data onto the CD-ROM or DVD for download to computer systems. In terms of speed, DVDs are faster than CD-ROMs, and Blue Ray disks are the fastest of all. Both DVDs and CD-ROMs can be either R or RW. DVD-R or CD-ROM-R is read only; data cannot be written to this type of DVD or CD-ROM. DVDs and CD-RWs can not only contain data but data and information can be written to them.

*Monitors*

For desktop computers the two most common types of monitors are cathode ray tube displays (CRTs) or liquid crystal displays (LCDs). LCD monitors are also referred to as flat panel monitors. LCD monitors have taken the CRT out of the monitor market. LCD monitors are lighter in weight and have a smaller footprint than CRT monitors. Furthermore, they use less energy and are cheaper than CRT monitors. Keep in mind that either of these types of monitors can be attached to a notebook computer. CRT monitors are similar to a regular TV set. You may be asked what the optimum size is for a monitor for a computer system. As a general rule monitors should not be less than 17 inches; 15-inch monitors are very difficult for students to read.

*Sound Devices*

One of the things your students will want to do is to listen to sound from their computer systems. This can range from music, to streaming video, to podcasts. In a home computer system a set of speakers provides sound output. Depending on the needs of the system user, the speaker system can be very sophisticated. In a school library situation, however, you will probably want to use headphones with any sound system. If the system is used in a classroom or larger area, an amplifier may be required.

## Printers

Printers have always have been the primary output devices for computer systems. As mentioned earlier, one of the early goals of technology and computer systems was to achieve some sort of paperless system. We know now this goal has failed, and, if possible, we print more than we ever have, and this is considering just the intentional printing of documents. What I mean is printing that was meant to be done. All too often printers are the weakest part of a computer system, and our students prove it every day. If they send a print command and no paper comes out, do they think something is wrong? No, they just continue to send print commands. When whatever issue the printer had is fixed, out come multiple copies of the same thing. What a waste of paper!

For our purposes we will consider three types of printers: impact printers, inkjet printers, and laser printers. Impact printers, more commonly known as dot-matrix printers, are rapidly becoming legacy items except in business offices where large masses of printing must be done. Impact printers are still the cheapest way to print, but either they do not print graphics or they print them very crudely.

The printer of choice, both for cost and quality, in home computer systems, is the inkjet printer. Inkjet printers vary widely in both price and print quality. Inkjet printers have decreased in price to the point that it is not cost-effective to repair them. They are just discarded and replaced. The major expense associated with inkjet printers is the cost of ink cartridges. Inkjet printers are often not the best choice for school libraries because of this cartridge cost and the fact that they often turn into color photocopiers, with users producing multiple color copies at will.

The most efficient type of printer that is available for the school library is the laser printer. While the initial cost for high-quality laser printers is greater than for inkjet or dot-matrix printers, the cost in lifespan of toner cartridges makes laser printers the best solution for heavy-duty library printing. Laser printers use laser beams and static electricity to place an image on paper. Laser printers are quick, quiet, and produce high-quality printouts.

When you are making the decision as to what printers you want in your school library there are several points to consider. First, the speed of the printer. Print speeds generally range from eight to thirty pages per minute. Always remember that printing text is faster than printing graphics. The second consideration is the printers' resolution. This is the printed character's clarity and is measured in dots per inch (dpi). As a general rule the higher the resolution, the more expensive and slower the printer. Think about what your library's printers will be used for when considering the acceptable resolution. The third consideration is color output. If you are committed to having at least some color printing capability in your library, you will have to decide if you want an inkjet or a color laser printer. Printers need internal memory in order to print. You must determine what your printers will be used for when determining how much memory is required. Inkjet printers can slow to a crawl if they do not have enough memory, while laser printer will just not print if they do not have enough memory. Carefully look at your printing needs. If you are printing mostly text documents, a laser printer is probably the best choice. If you have a requirement for high-quality color graphics, then an inkjet printer is probably the best choice. The final consideration when evaluating printers is the cost of consumables.

A type of printer that is gaining popularity with home computer users is the all-in-one printer. An all-in-one printer combines the functions of a printer, scanner, copier, and fax into one machine. They can be valuable in the library offices because they save space, but they should be used with caution in the public areas of the school library because they have capabilities you may not want to make available.

One final concept of printing that needs to be considered is centralized printing. As was discussed earlier, much paper can be wasted in a school library because there is a lack of awareness of malfunctions of printers that can cause this wasting of paper. A way to solve this is to centralize printing. This allows monitoring of printers and, it is hoped, a minimum of wasted paper. While it often takes a dedicated worker to monitor the centralized printing, this cost can be matched by the savings from paper that is not wasted.

## Scanners

At one time it was thought scanners and the scanning process would become one of the primary input modes for computers. For several reasons this has not proved true. Scanning can be a complicated process and often does not yield results or the quality desired. Scanners can scan graphics and text. When you scan graphics they can then be manipulated using graphics or drawing programs. Text can be scanned and then converted using optical character recognition (OCR) software. OCR software is designed to simplify the conversion of text material for use with a word processing program. This is a complicated process. If the user does not have a nearly perfect copy of the text, cleaning up after the scan can take an inordinate amount of time. A skilled typist can enter text more rapidly than OCR software can accurately convert text if the copy is at all flawed. It is true that scanners have become less expensive and a bit easier to use, but the most commonly used application for scanners is in large-scale digitization projects, such as the Google book digitization project.

This introduction to computer peripherals is basic but provides school librarians with some fundamental knowledge that will be valuable. Other computer peripherals are out there, but the ones described here are the most commonly used. By the time you are reading this there could well be several other types of computer peripherals available.

## STUDENT COMPUTERS

Trying to determine what kind of computers should be available for students in the school library, how many are needed, and determining how they will be financed are key questions the school librarian must address. Further along in the chapter we will discuss the different types of computers available for student use and discuss in some detail the technical specifications for the "ideal" student computer.

When trying to decide how many computers are the ideal for your school library the driving force is how much money is available. You always have to take into consideration the dollars. In an ideal world, each user of the school library would have a computer with an Internet connection and a work area. This is the ideal, however. The reality is often less than that, even to the point of having only one computer. You will have to determine what your situation will bear.

One of the aspects you will have to resolve is if you (your library) or your district will purchase computers or lease them. This will depend to a great degree on the source of funds for technology. If the funds are onetime or will be bonded it may make the most sense to purchase computers. This is not a decision that should be made precipitously because purchasing means a large initial outlay for computers that will all become outdated and need to be replaced at one time.

Leasing provides you with some flexibility with computer procurement but it requires a constant funding stream because there will be payments required each year. The advantage to leasing is that you can plan for phased replacement of computers each year with a less substantial outlay of funds. In summary then, if you have onetime funding, purchasing computers is probably the best option, while if you have a steady funding stream leasing is a smarter option.

## TYPES OF STUDENT COMPUTERS

In this section we will take a quick tour through the different kinds of computers that might be available to your students. These types include desktop computers, laptop or notebook computers, tablet computers, handheld devices, and a new entry into the student computer field, the netbook computer. Each one of these computers has varying degrees of power and a wide variety of uses. In general, there are two basic computer platforms, Windows computers and Macintosh computers. At one time Apple computers were preeminent in the field of education, but that has changed over the past ten years with Windows-based computers now taking a lead. While we all recognize Dell and Gateway as the leading manufacturers of Windows-based computers, there is no one manufacturer that is predominant in the field.

### Desktop Computers

For several reasons, desktop computers of some kind are the most common computers used in education, no matter if it is elementary school or college. First, when considering the capability and power of computers, desktop computers are the most economical. The same power that you might find in a desktop computer, if placed in a notebook computer, would be significantly more expensive. Second, desktop computers are easy to expand and update. Furthermore, expansion and upgrading a desktop computer is relatively unlimited compared to other types of computers.

Desktop computers are generally the machine of choice for school libraries because they easily accept peripheral devices and are, as mentioned before, relatively cost-effective. A drawback when using desktop computers in a school library is that they are more difficult to move than other types of computers and take more space if you want to change the configuration of the library.

### Notebook Computers

Notebook, or laptop computers, put the computer CPU, monitor, mouse, and keyboard in one unit, giving users a large amount of flexibility as to where they will compute. As notebook computers have evolved over the years, they have become lighter and more compact and at the same time more powerful. Another factor that has made notebook computers more popular is the proliferation of wireless networks. Instead of being tied to a desktop computer with a wired network connection, a notebook with a wireless network connection allows a student to work where they want as long as the battery in the notebook lasts and they are in range of the wireless network.

Several states and many school districts have initiatives to give each school student a notebook computer. One of the first school districts to successfully implement a notebook giveaway program was the Greater Latrobe School District in Latrobe, Pennsylvania. In several of these programs the notebook computers given to the students are not full capability laptops but rather are special computers with some limits to their capability. While programs of this sort can be very costly, they do overcome the issue of equity that can occur when there is a great deal of computer software and information for student use but not every student has access to a computer.

When weighing the use of notebook computers in the school library, there are a few drawbacks. The first of these is the cost. On a per unit basis, notebook computers are significantly more expensive then desktop computers. Second, the very portability that makes them so attractive to students also means that they can very easily "get legs" and disappear. While notebook computers are probably not the first choice for widespread student use in the school library, they do fill some computing needs.

### Tablet Computers

Tablet computers make up a very small part of the computers sold, though they are gaining some popularity. Tablet computers are in effect a notebook computer with the additional user capability of interacting with software using a stylus to tap on the tablet screen. Tablet computers also have the software capability to convert what is written on the tablet to word processed text. This capability has existed in other hardware for some time, but tablet computers are a step forward in sophistication.

### Handheld Devices

As we move forward into the twenty-first century, the use of handheld computing devices is becoming much more common. In fact, this may be the answer to every student having a computer. Handheld devices might be a PDA such as a Palm or a Blackberry, or a cell phone such as the Apple iPhone. In each case the device allows access to the Web and e-mail and also provides a utility program similar to Microsoft Office and a basic operating system. It is well to keep in mind that a PDA has more computing power than NASA did when they put a man on the moon.

### Netbooks

The final computer to consider is the netbook or a sub-notebook as it is also called. A netbook is a small computer (about one-third the size of a notebook computer) that provides nearly as much computer capability as a full-size notebook computer. A netbook normally sells for less than $300 but provides full access to the Internet and to e-mail. They typically use the LINUX operating system and Open Office as opposed to Microsoft Office as the productivity software. Netbooks are very prevalent in Europe and Asia and are just beginning to catch on in the United States.

### Specifications for Student Computers

I hesitate to include typical specifications for student computers because as soon as one reads them they are out of date. Nevertheless I will suggest two sets of specifications for student computers, a minimum set and the preferred set.

**Computer Specifications**

| Feature | Minimum | Recommended |
|---|---|---|
| Processor | Intel 1.66 GHz | Intel 2.4 GHz |
| Memory | 2 GB | 4 GB |
| Hard Disk | 80 GB | 250 GB |
| Optical Drive | CD-RW/DVD | DVD-RW |
| Network | Built in LAN 10/100 Wireless for laptops | Built in LAN Gigabit Wireless for laptops |
| Video Ram | 128 MB | 256 MB |
| Operating System | Windows 7 Mac OS X | Windows 7 Mac OS X |
| Software | Microsoft Office | Microsoft Office |

# SOFTWARE

Several different categories of software for the library computers will be discussed in this chapter. These categories include operating systems, productivity software, browser software, Web development software, antivirus software, and spyware. All of these categories of software are of importance to the school librarian, but every application does not have to be on every computer with the exception of operating system software. As you examine this list of categories of software, you may notice two categories are missing. The first is educational software such as drill and practice and simulations. While this book is attempting to be as comprehensive as possible, the topic of educational software used primarily in the classroom is beyond its scope. The second category of software not described in this chapter is library management software. This category will be discussed in much greater detail in Chapter 6. Software changes almost as rapidly as hardware. While the inclination is always to have the newest and most powerful software, it is not always necessary.

## *Operating Systems*

The operating system of a computer is the system software that controls how a user interacts with the computer. Its functions include the management of the computer hardware, computer software, and the computer peripherals. In the early days of personal computers in school libraries, the type of computer or platform used determined which operating system was used. This remains the case today. Again, in the early days of computing if you were using Apple computers in your school library, you were using some version of the Apple operating system. If you had IBM or compatible computers, you used a Disk Operating System (DOS). The DOS system resembled a terminal based operating system as commands were typed in at a prompt to cause operations to occur. What we will discuss here are graphic user interface (GUI) operating systems we are generally familiar with. We will examine Microsoft Windows, the Mac Operating System, and Linux.

*Microsoft Windows*

Microsoft Windows is the base operating system for most non-Apple Macintosh computers used in school libraries. Windows has gone through many upgrades and improvements since its introduction as Windows 3.1. The most current version of Windows is Vista, introduced to replace Windows XP. This roll-out was perhaps precipitous as there are a number of issues with Vista that are well publicized in the media. Microsoft has worked hard to solve these problems with improvements called patches, but a number of businesses and educational institutions have elected to stay with Window XP and not move to Windows Vista despite the fact that Microsoft has announced the end of support for Windows XP. The major difference between these two versions of Windows is that Windows XP was built around features, while Windows Vista is built around users. This is perhaps best shown in the table below which compares Windows XP and Windows Vista versions:

| **Vista Version** | **Description** | **Windows XP Version** |
| --- | --- | --- |
| Vista Home Basic | Basic, low-budget operating system | XP Home Edition |
| Vista Home Premium | Combines the media features of XP Home Edition and XP Media Center Edition | XP Home Edition with features from XP Media Center Edition |
| Vista Business | Aimed at the business market | XP Professional |
| Vista Enterprise | Not available in retail stores; aimed at a niche business market | |
| Vista Ultimate | Top-of-the-line operating system. Aimed at application developers. | |

*Macintosh Operating System*

The Mac OS functions only on Apple Macintosh computers with no compatibility between Windows and Apple computers even though the operating systems are very similar in appearance and functionality. In 1984 the Mac OS was introduced with the Macintosh computer. The Mac OS was the first commercially available operating system with a graphic user interface, or GUI. This allowed users to have a point-and-click interface not available with DOS operating system computers. It took the introduction of Microsoft Windows to achieve this same point and click graphical user interface to other types of computers. Over the years the Macintosh with the Mac OS has become a niche machine, generally used for graphics applications. Mac OS users are a loyal group and point to the system's greater system reliability. Furthermore, the Mac OS is nearly invulnerable to viruses. Because the Macintosh is a niche machine, there are far fewer software applications available.

## Linux

As users in business, education, and at home have become less satisfied with either Microsoft Windows or the Mac OS, more have turned to the Linux operating system. Linux is an example of open source software that is available for developers to use or modify. The reputation of Linux is that it is more stable than other operating systems and is far less apt to crash. Because it is open source software, it is easy to change or modify to meet any developments in operating systems. Linux is an operating system that in its basic form can be downloaded for free. Other versions of Linux do have charges and fees associated with them, and they also provide support and other features that are not available with the free versions of Linux.

## Productivity Software

Productivity software is the real core of computing for many users. It is, in the educational arena, software that produces research papers, creates grade books, produces attractive presentations, and allows for the creation and manipulation of databases. More specifically, productivity software generally includes word processing software, spreadsheet software, presentation software, and database software. Each type of application is available from several manufacturers and for all computer platforms. All of these applications have their genesis in mainframe computer applications and have evolved for the personal computer.

As time passed, users looked for productivity software that integrated all of these pieces into one software package, called a "suite" of software. The first integrated software suite available to the educational user was Appleworks, which was developed for the Apple II family of computers. Since then there have been many software suites developed, but the most commonly used productivity software suite today is Microsoft Office. It is widely used in education and is really the standard productivity software. It is taught in nearly all educational institutions and is widely used in educational administration. Microsoft Office, in its most popular configuration, consists of Microsoft Word for word processing, Microsoft Excel, the spreadsheet component, Microsoft PowerPoint, the presentation software component, and Microsoft Access, the package's relational database. The interface of these components is so tightly interwoven that, for example, if an Excel chart is placed in a Word document, when the Excel data is changed, so is the chart placed in Word. At once praised and criticized, Microsoft Office really tries to be all things to all users. This has, in turn, created an extremely powerful program, but one that the average computer user will only scratch the surface of its power.

Two other software suites that deserve mention are Microsoft Works and WordPerfect Suite. Both have shipped preloaded on personal computers at different times and were billed as lower-cost alternatives to Microsoft Office. Microsoft Works was widely used in education because of its lower cost and simplicity of use. While having fewer features than Microsoft Office, Microsoft Works was generally viewed as easier to use. One major drawback to Microsoft Works, however, was a nearly total lack of compatibility between Microsoft Office and Microsoft Works. It was not, for example, possible to open a Works word-processed document in Word. Databases created in Works could not be opened in Access. This lack of compatibility was a major drawback for the Microsoft Works user.

The other productivity suite mentioned was WordPerfect Suite. This is software based on the WordPerfect interface and was shipped at no additional cost on many personal computers. While the software is robust and user-friendly, WordPerfect Suite has the same drawback as does Microsoft Works: it is not compatible with Microsoft Office, an absolute requirement when Microsoft Office is the standard.

A third productivity suite recently on the scene is Open Office. Like Linux, Open Office is open source software and can be downloaded for free from the Internet. Open Office has a great deal of compatibility with Microsoft Office, but it takes a relatively experienced computer user to get the compatibility right. Open Office can be used with a Windows, a Macintosh, or a Linux operating system computer.

### Communication Software

Three types of communication software will be discussed: IM or instant messaging software, chat software, and e-mail software. Actually IM is not software but a service that allows one to communicate with others online the same time you are. Rather than allowing relatively unfiltered communications as chat software does, IM requires a predefined list of contacts before you can send or receive messages.

Chat rooms, which use chat software, are a type of synchronous (real-time) communication that occurs when conversation is real-time and all parts of the conversation are visible to everyone else in the chat room.

Although not a hard and fast rule, chat rooms are generally organized around a single theme or topic. It was felt at one time that the concept of chat and chat rooms would just be a computing fad that would be popular for a short period of time and then disappear. This has not proved to be the case as the topicality of chat has helped it remain popular.

Before moving to e-mail software, some discussion of the pros and cons of chat and IM synchronous communications in the library or education setting is necessary. As a rule, schools do not permit either IM or chat anywhere on school networks. Districts feel there is too much risk and too much wasted time when they are permitted. In truth there can be cogent educational reasons to allow synchronous communications, particularly chat, if there is close teacher or librarian supervision. An example of using chat in an educational setting is the formation of study groups for AP courses. Again, it has to be directed and supervised by a teacher or school librarian.

Today in schools and libraries the first thing we want to do when we sit down at a computer is check our e-mail. To give it a definition, e-mail is a type of Internet-based communication in which people correspond. E-mail is an example of asynchronous communication in which the sender and receiver of e-mail do not have to be available at the same time to correspond. E-mail has achieved great popularity because it is fast and convenient and saves postage and phone bills. A recent survey showed that 80 percent of Americans who use the Internet use it primarily for e-mail.

Two different methods of using e-mail include client-based e-mail, which requires local installation of e-mail software, and Web-based e-mail, which only requires a Web browser. Most e-mail done in schools and school libraries is client-based e-mail, and the e-mail software resides on all district computers. In many cases school district e-mail users can also access their e-mail from home and school through Web-based e-mail. The big advantage to using Web-based e-mail is that you can access the mail from any computer at any time.

If you are using client-based e-mail, chances are good your e-mail software is Microsoft Outlook. Microsoft Outlook is a powerful e-mail software package that also includes a robust calendaring and scheduling feature. Versions of Microsoft Windows prior to Vista included a more basic e-mail package called Outlook Express. For many e-mail users this was all the capability they needed for e-mail.

Before leaving the topic of e-mail, all school librarians, teachers, and in fact all e-mail users need to understand that there is no inherent right to privacy with e-mail. The courts have found that e-mail does not carry with it the same right to privacy as the U.S. mail, particularly when an employer's e-mail system is used. All e-mail users must be aware of this and be wary when using e-mail.

### Antivirus Software

Antivirus software is software designed to detect viruses that are attempting to attack a computer and protect the computer and its files from harm. Other than the operating system, which allows the computer to function, no other type of software is as necessary as antivirus software. No computer in your school library should be without antivirus software, and it is essential to keep it up-to-date as new viruses are circulated every day.

A virus is a computer program, generally brought in through the Internet, that attaches itself to other computer programs and attempts to spread to other computers when files are exchanged. A very few viruses can be harmless, but the vast majority want to harm a computer or computer files. For example, a virus that you download might erase the hard drive of your computer. As mentioned before, having antivirus software on your computer, keeping it updated, and regularly scanning your computer system for viruses is essential.

### Graphics Software

The growth in the different types of graphics software made available in the last ten years has been great. If you want to make graphics software available on your computers in the library, you will want to consider a drawing software program and a photo editing program. There are a number of good drawing programs available, so you will want to consult with the art department in your school to determine what their preference is.

As far as photo editing is concerned, one of the most commonly used pieces of software is Photoshop. The full version of Photoshop has a very steep learning curve and is quite expensive, so you might want to consider its less robust version, Photoshop Lite. If you are going to provide an environment in your school library in which students are going to work on projects, then graphics software is a must.

### Internet Browsers

Two things are required for the computers in your school library to connect to the Internet: an Internet service provider (ISP) and browser software. Web browser software allows users to locate items on the Web and to navigate the Web. The most common browsers in use today are Microsoft Internet Explorer, Mozilla Firefox, and a new entry in the arena, Google Chrome. Each of these browsers has its proponents and its opponents. School districts generally standardize on one browser so other than providing opinion and input you may not be able to make the final decision. When you are working with Internet browsers there are a couple of things to keep in mind; first, the same Web page may display differently in different browsers, and second, monitor settings can also affect the way Web pages display.

### Web Development Software

School librarians have three approaches to creating Web pages. The first is to use hypertext markup language (HTML) and create pages using this code. For more experienced Web page developers, this is the method of choice because it provides absolute control over the appearance of the Web page. The second approach to creating Web pages, particularly if just one or a few Web pages are created and there is no need for a full-blown Web site, is to create documents in different applications such as Microsoft Word and then convert the documents to Web pages.

Falling somewhere between these two approaches is the use of Web page authoring software. The use of Web page software eliminates the need for programming skills when creating Web pages but at the same time allows for the creation of complex Web sites relatively easily. This type of software generally includes wizards, reference pages, and templates that will help the user in creating Web pages and Web sites. The most widely used Web development software packages are Adobe Dreamweaver and Microsoft Expression Web. Expression Web has replaced Microsoft FrontPage, although you will still find FrontPage in many education environments. Although these software packages do make the creation of Web pages and Web sites easier, they both have high learning curves and are not particularly intuitive.

### Spyware Removal Software

Spyware is generally not particularly dangerous when it is downloaded to your computer, but it can be very bothersome. Spyware is a program that is downloaded from the Internet to your computer along with software you have meant to download. Many spyware programs use cookies to collect information on what is used on your computer, while other spyware records keystrokes with the aim of stealing passwords, logins, or credit card information. In order to control and remove spyware form your computer, you will want to install anti-spyware software. If you are using Windows Vista, it has a built-in anti-spyware program titled Windows Vista Defender. If you are using operating systems there are anti-spyware programs that can and should be installed. Because there is new spyware created daily you should keep your anti-spyware up to date and run it frequently.

## CONCLUSION

Chapter 3 discussed networks, computer hardware, and computer software. Some school librarians would question the value of this material to their jobs, but if the librarian is to be a technology leader in their school, it is essential knowledge. Of the many areas covered in this book, the material in this chapter is the most likely to change rapidly, and it requires a dedication to professional development to stay current with the computer technology.

Chapter 4 presents an in-depth discussion of planning for technology in the school and the school library. Planning is the key to getting technology—it takes more than "I really could use more computers" to get technology. It must be planned for and be related to student achievement.

## RESOURCES

American Library Association. "AASL Information Power Action Research Project." ALA. http://www.ala.org/ala/mgrps/divs/aasl/aaslproftools/informationpower/informationpower.cfm (accessed January 11, 2009).

Bilal, Dania. *Automating Media Centers and Small Libraries: A Microcomputer-Based Approach*. Greenwood Village, CO: Libraries Unlimited, 2002.

Burke, John J. *Neal-Schuman Library Technology Companion: A Basic Guide for Library Staff*. New York: Neal-Schuman, 2004.

Cohn, John M., Ann L. Kelsey, and Keith Michael Fields. *Planning for Integrated Systems and Technologies: A How-To-Do-It Manual for Librarians*. New York: Neal-Schuman, 2001.

"Colorado Technology Competency Guidelines for Classroom Teachers and School Library Media Specialists." ERIC. http://www.eric.ed.gov/ERICWebPortal/custom/portlets/recordDetails/detailmini.jsp?_nfpb=true&_&ERICExtSearch_SearchValue_0=ED433020&ERICExtSearch_SearchType_0=no&accno=ED433020 (accessed January 14, 2009).

Doggett, Sandra L. *Beyond the Book: Technology Integration into the Secondary School Library Media Curriculum*. Englewood, CO: Amy Landecker: Libraries Unlimited, 2000.

Evans, Alan, Kendall Martin, and Mary Ann Poatsy. *Go! Technology in Action*. Upper Saddle River, NJ: Amy Landecker Prentice Hall, 2010.

Farkas, Meredith. "Skills for the 21st Century Librarian." http://meredith.wolfwater.com/wordpress/2006/07/17/skills-for-the-21st-century-librarian/ (accessed January 14, 2009).

Jurkowski, Odin L. *Technology and the School Library: A Comprehensive Guide for Media Specialists and Other Educators*. Lanham, MD: Scarecrow, 2006.

Kochtanek, Thomas R., and Joseph R. Matthews. *Library Information Systems: From Library Automation to Distributed Information Access Solutions*. Westport, CT: Amy Landecker: Libraries Unlimited, 2002.

Lowe, Carrie. "The Role of the School Library Media Specialist in the 21st Century." Eric Digest. http://www.ericdigests.org/2001-3/21st.htm (accessed January 14 2009.

Matthews, Joseph R. *Technology Planning: Preparing and Updating a Library Technology Plan*. Westport, CT: Amy Landecker: Libraries Unlimited, 2004.

NCLIS. "School Libraries Work." http://www2.scholastic.com/content/collateral_resources/pdf/s/slw3_2008.pdf Accessed January 14, 2009).

Turner, Laura. "20 Technology Skills Every Educator Should Have." http://www.instructor.aviation.ca/content/view/133/71 (accessed January 14, 2009).

Williams, Brad. *We're Getting Wired, We're Going Mobile, What's Next? Fresh Ideas for Educational Technology Planning*. Eugene, OR: Amy Landecker: ISTE, 2004.

# QUESTIONS FOR RESEARCH AND DISCUSSION

1. Chapter 3 discussed several reasons for having your school library networked. The alternative is stand-alone machines. Please explain why it is a good plan for the school library to be part of both a local area network and a wide area network. Are there any drawbacks? Incorporate the latest research into your response.

2. Microsoft Office is the standard for productivity software used in both businesses and schools, but Open Office is seen by some as a viable alternative. Research both packages and prepare a presentation that you would give to your Technology Coordinator supporting the purchase of one or another. Remember that you may inject your opinion, but it must be supported by facts and research.

3. Your superintendent has asked you to consider the use of thin client technology in your school library as a way to contain costs. Your report to him should compare and contrast thin and fat client technology, bringing out the strong and weak points of each. Arrive at a conclusion concerning the use of thin client technology that is in the best interests of your school library.

4. One of the most important parts of hardware planning for the school library is the specifications for the computers that will be used in your school library. Prepare a plan for replacing the computers currently in your school library with machines that will accomplish all the technology requirements you will have. Be sure and consider all parts of the computer and include costs for the computers. Keep in mind the possible need for further expansion.

5. Several network topologies were discussed in the chapter. Analyze each of these topologies and compare and contrast them. Determine which would be the best fit for your school and your school library.

6. An issue that often faces school librarians with relation to technology is to recommend buying computers or leasing them. Research the topic, including contacting school districts that procure computers both ways and prepare a position paper discussing which is the most effective method for procuring computers. Consider the method of funding and the long-term costs.

# 4

# *Planning for Technology in the School Library*

In the last two chapters we have discussed the technology skills that the twenty-first-century school librarian should possess and have provided an overview of hardware and software that may be appropriate to use in the school library. In this chapter we will examine in depth the technology planning process that should be used in the school library. At first glance the reader would think this chapter is not necessary for either of two reasons. For some the need for technology is so obvious, planning for it and justifying its purchase is superfluous and unneeded. For others, the need for detailed planning and providing justification for purchasing technology is so similarly necessary describing it is not necessary.

Let me make two things clear. First, no superintendent or school board ever recognizes the need to spend money without prior planning and justification. This is just a law of nature. Second, the more thorough and transparent the planning process, the more likely it is the plan will be approved.

In some states the technology planning process has become a part of the formal strategic planning process completed periodically in order to meet state requirements. This is currently the case in Pennsylvania. Other states have adopted an electronic, "cookie cutter" approach to technology planning. In these cases everyone's technology plan is based on a predesigned template so all technology plans look essentially alike. An example of this was the ETech Planner tool formerly used in Pennsylvania. Finally, some states allow technology plans to be created using some general guidelines but do not use a common template.

# WHAT A TECHNOLOGY PLAN CAN BE

What is your responsibility as a school librarian in the technology planning process? If you expect to have technology in your library, you had better be right in the middle of the process. It is easy for us to say planning for technology is someone else's responsibility, but that is a sure recipe not to have any technology in your library. For a library technology plan you may want to consider some of the following.

One of the areas that modern school librarians need to be concerned with is the procurement of electronic content. A corollary of electronic content acquisition is the creation of electronic content for the school library. This process typically would include the creation of descriptive cataloging and the creation of digital collections. The final area to be considered for a library technology plan is infrastructure. This includes user support for instruction, library office, and IT and networking issues.

A technology plan's content depends on what it is to be used for. Your school library technology plan can be used to obtain ERate and state funds. Nearly all procurement of funds such as ERate and state and federal funds require a technology plan be approved and be on file in order to obtain the funding. A school library technology plan can take one of three forms. First, and most typical in school districts, it is part of a larger organization technology plan such as the school district's technology plan. Second, it can be part of the library's overall plan. This most often occurs in school districts with multiple libraries and a library department chair or supervisor. Third, the library's technology plan can stand alone.

# EFFECTIVE TECHNOLOGY PLANNING

If you have some freedom in the format your school technology plan will take, there are some considerations to include in the planning process. Of course if you are using an existing template many of these items will be beyond your control.

- The most effective technology plans are short term, not long term. Too often your school district will want a five-year technology plan. Resist this! Remember Moore's Law! In some cases we cannot predict what technology will be available in one year, much less five years. For this reason you may want to tie your technology plan to phases, not years.

    If your school district insists on a longer term technology plan, correlate it with the district's budget process. Review the technology plan each year it is in force during the budget process to make sure you are not buying old or outmoded technology. It is important in this regard to keep in mind that a technology plan should be dynamic and not lock you into old technology and applications.

- The most effective technology plans are based on applications, not the technology itself. This seems counterintuitive to say a technology plan is not based on technology, but it should be true. Rather than your technology plan being a lengthy list of hardware and software you want, the plan should say what you want your stakeholders to be able to do with technology and then let the objectives and outcomes determine what and how much technology will be required to meet the goals.

  Often when technology plans are presented to school boards, the first question the board will ask is how will the technology be used? If the plan is written addressing what students and teachers will be able to do with the technology, the question is answered within the plan itself. Having the technology plan focus on technology outcomes can also help to defuse debates about standardizing on a particular brand or platform. While some standardization can be positive and cost-effective, the hardware and applications purchased should be driven by what will most effectively meet the objectives specified in the technology plan. The whole issue of standardization should not be a major issue today as modern networks can easily work with different platforms.

- The technology plan should go beyond just enhancing the curriculum. It must be kept in mind that the real goal of the technology plan is to allow the stakeholders to work easier, not harder. Far too many technology plans want to use technology to teach about technology. We have only to look at schools that have defined "computer classes" taught by a "computer teacher." This is just wrongheaded. After all, is it more important for students to be able to use technology to find reference or resource material or to insure they have the right fingers on the right keys on a keyboard? It seems as though we are killing ants with a sledgehammer when we teach keyboarding on a computer when there are much more economical, practical solutions available. Look around—there might even be some typewriters stored in your school that could be used to teach keyboarding.

- Remember that there is more to technology than just computers. The most effective technology plans deal with the entire gamut of technology, not just computers. It might include photography equipment, television equipment, and even video-conferencing equipment and the software to support the equipment. When the technology plan is completed, it must include all types of technology.

- Integration of technology into the curriculum makes a technology plan more effective. This relates closely to Item 3, above. Teachers and librarians often rightfully ask why they have to stop teaching their subjects in order to teach technology. Above all, technology is a tool used to assist learning, not be the objective of the learning itself. Often when we teach technology, students will work with a piece of software to learn all the capabilities of the software. If you are integrating the use of the software into another lesson, is it not enough to teach the students only what they need to know about the software to complete the lesson, not the complete software package?
- It is imperative that technology plans be closely tied to staff-development plans. If they are not, they are doomed to fail. For many years, the solution for technology for teachers was to wheel it in and leave it. No training. Apparently teachers and school librarians are expected to learn to use technology by osmosis. What occurs when this is the case is to create really expensive doorstops.

  Staff development or training can be looked at as four steps: awareness, application, integration, and refinement. In most cases teachers are rarely beyond the awareness level as in "yes, that is a computer." The goal of an effective technology plan is to attempt to move those at the awareness level as far up the continuum as possible. Not everyone will be able to move to the refinement level, but that should be the goal. Too often the conversation between two teachers at the refinement level causes those at the awareness level to just roll their eyes as a sign of not understanding.
- Technology plans make technology the cost of doing business; money and time are available for technology. For example, is it necessary for every student to have a hard copy of a textbook? Would it be possible to only purchase classroom sets of textbooks and use the money that remains to purchase instructional resources for the school library? Let us take this a step further: Is a textbook necessary at all? Is it possible to move to a resource-based learning system and eliminate textbooks altogether? Some states are already discussing this possibility.

  Perhaps a new approach to training is also necessary. While the schools have the general responsibility for staff development and training, teachers and school librarians must take some responsibility also. Take that computer home and learn that new software and then come back and share with your teachers. Help them use the prep period to actually prep, not just as social time. Is this a new paradigm? Yes. Is it needed? Yes.
- Attributes of the technology plan should be based on research. It is easy to write a technology plan based on our gut feelings. It is harder,

but more valid, to base the conclusions in a technology plan on research.

- The users of a technology plan should be those who wrote it. Many times technology plans are developed by administrators or IT personnel who will not actually use much of the technology. One of the most effective technology initiatives I have had contact with was a technology proposal process. Staff members who wanted technology were required to write a proposal for what they wanted. The proposals were reviewed by the school district technology committee and then ranked. Technology proposals were then voted on, and those approved were funded.
- Focus on a vision. All good technology plans have a vision for technology. This vision should be the focus and aim of all technology in the plan. Never lose sight of the vision and you will be surprised how much progress you will make with technology.

As we move close to a discussion of the elements of an effective technology plan and the actual steps that should be followed in the construction of the technology plan, we need to consider why we need to do technology planning. In the larger picture nothing as important or costly as technology should be purchased without complete and thorough planning. Having said that, it is necessary to consider specific reasons or purposes for planning for technology. These purposes apply from the smallest school library to the largest school district. In many states there is no question about justifying the planning process: it is required by state mandate. Even if the technology planning is not mandated, it is still so important as to be required.

- The technology planning process should depict what the school librarian is currently doing with technology and what the library plans to do with new technology. As mentioned earlier, the aim should be how the technology will be integrated into the curriculum rather than just listing what the librarian wants without specifying how it will be used.
- The technology planning process should assist in the achievement of the technology vision. When we examine in detail the creation of the technology vision, you will see it is an integral part of the technology plan. The technology planning process should advance the achieving of the vision.
- The technology planning process should assist in managing the budget. Budget planning is a more cerebral process than many school librarians think. Budgeting is a matter of figuring out what the needs are and determining what is "nice to have." At times you will be able to get both; at other times you will only be able to meet your needs.

The technology planning process should go a long way toward seeing budget trends and realities.

- Current technology strengths and weaknesses can be easily identified through the technology planning process. One of the most important parts of the needs assessment is analyzing what is good about your current technology and what is bad. Only at that point can you begin to analyze what you need.
- New technology is always coming on the market, and sales personnel will be the first to tell you how much you need the new technology. The technology planning process will assist you in determining what of the new technology you need and how to prioritize your needs for new technology.
- Whether we call it training or staff development, it is always necessary to provide it for newly purchased technology. Teachers and librarians feel that needs are being ignored when they receive new technology and they are not trained in its use. The effective use of the technology planning process can help in the planning for training and the cost of that training must be included in the technology plan.
- The technology planning process can show how technology can be used effectively. One of the very important parts of the process is to show illustrations of the exemplary use of technology in the school library.
- One piece of the technology planning process that is often overlooked is creating a fund-raising plan. We always have a budget in technology plans, but we frequently do not indicate where the funds will come from. From this standpoint a fund-raising plan is essential.

Matthews (2004, 6–7) in his seminal work dealing with library technology planning, uses the acronym "SMART" to define what a technology plan should be. In his view a technology plan must be Specific, Measureable, Aggressive (but attainable), Results-oriented, and Time-bound.

## HOW NOT TO DO A TECHNOLOGY PLAN

Let us get this out of the way now—the things that can lead to a bad technology plan. While there are many, many ways to create a successful technology plan, there are also some things done in the name of technology planning that will inevitably lead to shortcomings in a technology plan. Ignore these at your own risk!

- Having only one, or at the most, two people write the technology plan the night before it is due raises two big areas of concern. First, a technology plan should never be created by one or two people; it should always be prepared by a committee representing all of the stakehold-ers. Second, it should go without saying that writing the technology plan the night before it is due is a certain recipe for disaster. Time is needed to review, confirming all the parts are in place and to add miss-ing elements while discarding the "nice to have" if it means losing the "must haves."

- Placing the technology coordinator in charge of the planning is too challenging. This person has more than enough work to do in their day-to-day routine to even think about taking charge of the planning, especially when this person's expertise is generally hardware or net-working. They often lack the broader perspective of technology in education or in the library. Often, you, as the school librarian, are the ideal choice to be in charge of the technology plan process.

- Keeping the plan a secret from the school or the community until it is completed. This is a cardinal sin because a plan without support will not be successful, and support cannot be accrued if some constituen-cies do not know what is in the plan.

- Making the technology plan is a shopping list of technology. All this does is allow your administration or school board to ask how the tech-nology will be used. Anticipate this and tie your technology plan to how students will have higher levels of achievement with technology.

- Ignoring the needs of the teachers and the librarians. This is a corol-lary to allowing the technology coordinator to prepare the technology plan. He or she is not an educator. Pay attention to what the teachers and librarians want and need.

- Forgetting to make accommodation for technology support. This is a fatal and very frustrating problem. School districts will rarely have the level of technology support found in industry, but not having a plan for technology support will lead to very high levels of frustration and closets full of broken or damaged equipment.

- Focusing on hardware, not curriculum integration in your technology plan. This relates to the shopping list concept described above.

In the above list we discussed some things guaranteed to make an unsuc-cessful technology plan. These ideas are pretty comprehensive, but below are four indications that a technology plan will not do what you and others hope it will do. First, as has been mentioned in several other places, the plan will focus on the technology itself rather than on how the technology will be used. If you cannot tie the technology to a specific curriculum or library use, you may want to rethink what you are asking for. The red flag should go up if your technology plan says something to the effect that the school library needs thirty computers, rather than, "In order to allow equity of access so students can research using electronic databases, the school library will need more computers."

Second, the plan does not clearly define how technology is being used in the library in support of your mission and technology vision. Your teachers and students are your customers. You need to explain how technology is being used to support their needs. Here a danger signal would be just explaining how teachers and the librarians are using technology rather than explaining how students are using it. The school board and your administrators will ask so you had better be ready to respond to them.

Third, the technology plan is so full of technology "nerd speak" and educational jargon it is unreadable by anyone except the those who wrote it. Too often this makes those who attempt to read it wary of what is there because they cannot understand it. The technology plan should be written in clear, understandable English; if it is not it should be revised.

Finally, not all important or pertinent information is included in the technology plan. If you are asking for computers that students can use to research using electronic databases and you do not define what databases they will use, then you are not providing all of the important and pertinent information.

## CREATING AN EFFECTIVE TECHNOLOGY PLAN

The germ for an idea for technology often begins with some questions you or one of your teachers may ask. These questions can be the starting point for technology planning and can frame the technology perceptions of teachers, administrators, and students. Among the questions are the following:

- Have you ever thought there has to be an easier way to do this?
- Have you ever thought I could do this faster if only . . . ?
- Have you ever thought I wish I had someone to help me do this?
- Have you ever thought I wish I had a computer or other device so I could . . . ?
- Have you ever thought I wish I or my students could contact someone right now to tell them . . . ?
- Have you ever thought I wish I or my students could contact someone right now to find out . . . ?
- Have you ever thought I wish my students had computers or other technological resources available so they could . . . ?
- Have you ever thought I wish my students had improved computers or other technological resources available so they could . . . ?
- Have you ever thought I wish my students had more computers or other technological resources so they could . . . ?

# RULES FOR TECHNOLOGY PLANNING

We have discussed in some depth what can make a technology plan bad or ineffective. In this section we will discuss some rules for successful technology planning. These are probably not rules in the accepted sense of the word, but they sure do make technology planning easier and more effective. It would be easy to say these should never be violated, but they are guidelines to help the school librarian.

- The technology plan should clearly resemble the technological maturity of the school or school district. What do we mean by this? It means that when you develop a technology plan, you have to consider the technology needs of every teacher and student, not just those who are technologically proficient. If all teachers and students had a high degree of technological proficiency, creating the plan would be easy. Unfortunately, they do not all have the same high level of proficiency. Think carefully about why the nonusers of technology in the school are nonusers. In other words, you have to look at the weakest and plan for them rather than planning for the strongest. If you do not do this, you will have parts of the school moving forward with technology while other parts are technology resistant. Keep this in mind as you go through the technology planning process; having the newest and best hardware and software does not necessarily indicate a technologically mature school. High-quality educational opportunities using technology do.
- *Resources require support!* This sentence is emphasized because it is so important in the technology planning process for the school and the school library. Many times technology plans are not thorough. You have asked for computers and software and have even indicated the educational necessity for these things in the plan, but you have not provided for furniture for the computers. Or you have not allowed for training on the new software. This is a sure formula for the software to be misused or not used at all. Similarly, when you have planned on a large scale for increasing the amount of technology in the school library and the IT department has only one person to maintain all of the computers in the school, you will have difficulty. The point is, either make sure there is support for what is in the plan or include the support in the plan.
- Do not confuse movement with change. Putting a computer on a teacher's desk is movement; getting that teacher or librarian to use that computer as a part of the educational process is change. In a similar manner, teachers and students can know how to use e-mail as a signal of movement, but when they are using e-mail for conferencing with people across the globe, you will see change. Change will not occur

magically or instantly. At the same time be sure to include measures of change in the plan and allow sufficient time for change to occur.

## MAKING TECHNOLOGY PLANNING WORTHWHILE

The technology plan is worthwhile if it achieves the goals set forth in the plan and it is focused on the learning and not just on the hardware and software. It is worthwhile if it establishes a connection between the learning taking place in the school library or classroom and the hardware and software. If the plan is to be worthwhile, it must be embraced by all the stakeholders in the school. With all of this said, there are still challenges to meet for the technology planning to be successful.

- You must have a vision for technology in your school library that is powerful and accounts for both teaching and learning. Many times when a technology plan is constructed, the vision statement is just an afterthought, something put together in a short period of time. This is really backward. The vision should be carefully and thoughtfully constructed so it is a true vision of what technology should be used for. All stakeholders should accept the vision, and it should guide all elements of the technology plan. Some schools go so far as to post the technology vision throughout the school.
- Have an established technology plan that is part of the overall improvement process in the school or school library. The technology plan is part of the assessment phase of the improvement program, and in this regard, it should do the following:
  - Assesses the current technology in use.
  - Communicates recommendations regarding technology.
  - Describes the projects and procedures that will implement the technology plan.
  - Indicates what resources will be needed to implement the technology plan.
  - Defines the technology capabilities that support learning.
- At this point the technology plan is submitted to the governing body for approval. If it is just a library technology plan it may go to the district technology committee. If it is a building or district technology plan, it will go to the school board. The governing body will, it is hoped, approve the plan and then set priorities and establish a funding stream for the plan.

  In the formulation phase of the improvement program, detailed specifications for the part of the technology plan are developed. At this point it may be necessary to consult with outside experts to insure the plan is feasible as written.

The implementation phase begins when the technology plan is approved and funded, when it becomes reality. The specifications developed in the formulation phase are the guides for the implementation of the technology plan.

- You must have or build support systems for the technology. This was discussed at some length previously, but it cannot be overemphasized. In nearly every school district I have visited the support system is so inadequate as to be laughable. I have seen cases in which a one-person IT department was responsible for more than 1,500 computers. This is simply an impossible task. Perhaps a warning anecdote is appropriate. A school district was attempting to hire a new director of IT and was quite impressed with an individual who was a network manager for a Fortune 500 company. This individual was eager to leave corporate life and move into an educational environment until two questions were asked. First question: in your current job situation how many people would be required to support 2,000+ computers? The answer: at least 20. Second question: how much money would it take to bring you to XYZ School District? The answer: it would have taken more money than the superintendent was paid. This may seem extreme, but this is the level of support prevalent in too many school districts. If this is the case in your district, changes have to be made, or technology will continue to be looked at as a tool that uses too much and delivers too little.
- Your training should explain how to use technology. Teachers and librarians want to know how to use hardware and software so they can integrate it into the curriculum. They do not want to know how the technology works. Most teachers and school librarians do not care how it works; they just care that it does work, and they want to know all of the ins and outs of making it effective in the curriculum. Forget the bits and bytes. Tell them how it works and how to use it in the classroom.
- You must support communication and collaboration among stakeholders. Not only is the technology plan developed by many stakeholders, it is shared with everyone involved in technology, including parents and students. Sharing the plan throughout makes it much easier to gain wide-ranging acceptance for the plan at the last meeting.

## INDICATIONS OF SUCCESSFUL TECHNOLOGY PLANNING FOR E-RATE FUNDING

Five criteria are the core elements for a technology plan to be approved for e-Rate funding (Writing a Library Technology Plan).

1. The plan should establish clear goals and a realistic strategy for using technology to improve instruction and administration in the education organization.
2. The plan should include an assessment of the hardware, software, networking, human resources, and financial resources needed to improve education services.
3. The plan should provide for a sufficient budget and schedule to acquire, maintain, and secure the hardware, software, and related issues (e.g., training) needed to implement the strategy.
4. The plan should have a professional development strategy to ensure staff members know how to use these new technologies to improve education services.
5. The plan should include an evaluation process that enables the organization to monitor progress toward the specified goals and make midcourse corrections in response to new developments and opportunities as they arise.

Furthermore, successful technology plans should address all or most of the following major areas:

- Current technology status and needs assessment
- Technology vision statements
- Equity issues
- Appropriate technology standards
- Integration into the curriculum
- Pilot program activities
- Infrastructure and support for infrastructure, including such facilities-related needs as air conditioning/cooling and asbestos abatement
- Review of current "state-of -the -art" technology for options in design of infrastructure
- Current capabilities of hardware and software
- Projections of "next-generation" capabilities and features
- Long-range goals
- Inventory control issues, such as maintenance and replacement cycle
- Budget projections and funding sources for initial installation, hardware, software, maintenance, security, and training
- Staff training
- Benchmarking standards
- Quality control components
- Security planning
- Evaluation planning
- Review cycles

When one is working with a technology plan, be it a school library technology plan or one for the entire school district, there are some other steps that should be considered. While they are not necessary in the strictest sense of the term, they do indicate the planning process has been carefully considered.

- A representative committee is in place. A technology plan should be a collaborative effort, not the work of one person. Furthermore, the committee should have a wide range of constituencies represented. It should not just include those teachers and administrators who are in favor of technology but should also include those who are less enthusiastic about technology and in particular should include parents and students.
- The committee should prepare one or more progress reports. The first should discuss where the school or library currently stands with relation to technology. This is the starting point for the technology plan. One or more progress reports during the planning process are also valuable because they keep stakeholders posted as to progress in the technology planning process.
- The responsibilities are subdivided among all members of the committee. It goes without saying there must be a chairman, but that chairman cannot do everything. Duties must be given to committee members based on their interests and/or their areas of expertise. The most difficult issue to deal with in this regard is the committee member who likes being on the committee but does not want to do anything. By subdividing the committee responsibilities, each member has a feeling of ownership and pride in the final technology plan.
- Time frames and due dates for tasks are established. It is important for time frames and due dates to be established for the report itself and for the subparts of the plan. In addition, there must be realistic, not some "pie-in-the-sky" time frame. When time frames have been established, it is incumbent on the chairman to insure they are met. This is a responsibility some chairmen find disagreeable, but it is necessary if the technology plan is to be completed in a timely manner.
- Consensus is built. If there is no consensus among all stakeholders on the final technology plan, the plan will never work. This sounds alarmist, but it is true. A technology plan approved by only a rump portion of the stakeholders will cause strife and disagreement not just on the committee, but in the school district as a whole. In this regard, consensus among taxpayers is an absolute necessity. They are the bill payers and must agree to the plan.

• The evaluation portion of the technology plan is formal and includes all stakeholders who helped develop the plan. Evaluation is key if the plan is to be effective and taken seriously within the community.

# CONSTRUCTING THE TECHNOLOGY PLAN

## School Library Technology Plans

From this point on, the discussion of technology plans is exclusively for the school library or the school library department. The place that most school library technology planning will begin is with the definition of the current state of library services and technology in the school library. Consider access to the content of local resources. Are students able to access them as needed, not just when they have a library permit? Are some resources restricted in use? These types of questions must be answered so issues of access can be dealt with.

Does the library have a portal to allow access to remote resources? One of the issues that will be discussed both later in this chapter and in Chapter 7 is the issue of the school library's Web presence and the quality of the Web page. If the school librarian does not have the skills to work with, this can be a serious problem area.

If electronic resources are to be accessed as needed, then there must be remote access to them. In other words, can the students access the electronic resources easily from home? This is a battle that the school librarian may well have to fight with the technology coordinator. IT personnel generally do not want to allow access through firewalls, and that is a requirement. The IT department may say this is impossible, but it is not and it must be done.

Human assistance is needed for everyone. This holds true even if the students are trying to access resources electronically and remotely. It may require a help desk setup or even flexible work hours, but having access to human assistance is very important.

## Building the Technology Environment

Building and improving the environment for technology in the school library is a very important but often overlooked aspect of the technology planning process in the school library. We have all heard the horror stories of computers ordered without furniture or of systems planned and ordered without adequate electrical outlets. These things seem so mundane but are so important. Among the issues from electricity to ergonomics to be considered are the following:

- Electricity. There are a whole gamut of electric issues. Are there enough outlets? Is the wiring adequate for the increased load? Can the power company provide upgrades if needed on a timely basis? The electric items are basic—technology runs on electricity.

- HVAC. While not as crucial as it was some time ago, technology requires a controlled environment. In particular, the area housing technology still requires air conditioning. Furthermore, the air conditioning system should be forced air, not water based. A water-based system puts too much moisture in the air for efficient use of technology.

- Cabling and Connections. Have these items been planned for? While it is often not possible for cabling to be in conduit when technology is placed in an existing school library, there are few thing worse than seeing cable laid under duct tape as is often the case. This is an area in which you really can use the help and expertise of your technology coordinator. This is what he or she is there to do, so use them!

- Carry-in Devices. This is an area of policy rather than environment. Are student and teacher devices such as personal notebook computers going to be allowed to be brought in? Think this issue through carefully and reach consensus on this policy.

- Lighting. Many school libraries do not have sufficient lighting for the effective use of technology. In this regard, the local power company will probably come to your facility to survey the lighting in the school library and tell you how it can be upgraded. In some ways lighting is as important as all of the other areas in considering the technology environment.

- Room and Layout. If the technology is in boxes in your library waiting to be unpacked and you do not know how you are going to configure the room, you are really behind the power curve! You should have planned the configuration of the room much earlier. How will the technology be supervised? Is the configuration efficient and conducive to good library usage? These are the types of things that have to be settled before the technology arrives.

- Furniture. Technology is here and you have not ordered furniture? The furniture is for high school students in your elementary library? The tables have arrived and there are no chairs? If there is no suitable furniture to hold the technology, the technology is useless.

- Ergonomics. This goes along with purchasing the correct furniture. Are the heights of the furniture correct for your students' use? Is the lighting correctly placed so there is no glare and the students can easily see the keyboards? Consider these and other ergonomic issues when building or changing the technology environment.

## *Updating an Existing Technology Plan*

It is not necessary to create a new technology plan from scratch every time. Once a technology plan has been created, the next time you consider the plan, you will update the existing plan, not create a new one. Some techniques you can use when it is time to update the technology plan include the following:

- Grade how effective the technology plan has been. This should not be just your opinion but should include the opinions of teachers, administrators, parents, and yes, students. The same people who were the stakeholders in the original plan should be the ones to grade it. Some among you might remember "Rate the Record" on the Dick Clark American Bandstand program in which kids would rate new records with such comments as "I give it a 90. You can dance to it." This is the type of anecdotal grading you might want from your students with regard to the existing technology plan.
- Get feedback from college students. Many times graduates of your school like to come back and lord it over the high school students. No matter if they are just a few months older, get these graduates to grade the old technology plan.
- Form a new review committee. Get a new slant on the technology plan by bringing in fresh faces. Sometimes this is easier said than done because there is some finite group of users who care about technology, but it is worth the effort to get new views.
- Get ideas from consumer technology shows. Sure, they are trying to sell you something, but this is an excellent way to gain ideas and knowledge about new and improved technologies.
- Readjust and maximize training. Has your training program been effective? If not, in the words of Madeline Hunter, "monitor and adjust." Do not continue ineffective training.
- See what other people are doing with technology in their school libraries. Get out of your library and go on the road. Many things go on with technology in school libraries; you just have to find them.
- Do a technology inventory. What you are really looking for is technology that is stashed in closets or storerooms because it is the technology found to be ineffective. Find out why it was ineffective and what could have been done to make it effective.
- Talk to those who question technology. This is very important. You get one picture from those who support technology but a far different view from those who question it. Take what they say seriously because if you do you may move them out of the questioning category.

- Get ideas about using technology in the school library from preservice programs. This may be difficult as the number of school library certification programs has shrunk, but if there is one in your area, visit it to get ideas.
- Incorporate technology into your curriculum plan. See if there are technology items in your state standards and adapt them into your curriculum plan. If you do not have a curriculum plan, you should and you need to get busy on it!

### Structure of the Technology Plan

The following is based on Joseph R. Matthews's (2004, 9–10) work on technology planning in the library. What follows are the elements of a library technology plan as they might be adapted for a school library. These ten elements are not magic, but they provide a framework for successful technology planning in the school library. Following are the elements in a successful library technology plan. Talking points developed by Matthews are included with the page numbers where they can be found.

1. Executive Summary (9). Although this is the first element listed, it actually is the last thing written. While we would like everyone who reads the technology plan to read every word, the reality is some will just not have the time and inclination to do so. The Executive Summary is for them. It will summarize all elements of the plan but not in great detail. An effective Executive Summary is typically between two and four pages.
2. Description of the Library (16–23). The description of the library should contain, as a minimum, the following elements:
   a. History. As a general rule the history of the school library is the same as the history of the school. It may also include a description of any renovations that have taken place.
   b. Physical Description. Nothing is more effective than a diagram of the school library and, because this is a technology plan, some digital photographs.
   c. The Library's Mission Statement. This is another thing that if you do not have one, do one, yesterday! You cannot be effective without a mission statement.
   d. Community Served. This should go beyond just a statement of how many students you serve in what grades. Consult the latest report from your regional accrediting agency for a detailed community profile.
   e. Staffing. Be sure to include nonprofessionals and vitae for all.

    f. Budget. Budget information should be detailed and include historical budget trends.

    g. Collection Size and Growth. You should be able to get this information from the reports section of your OPAC. The more detail you can provide the better.

    h. Services Offered. This section should be a complete list of what is done in the school library, why it is done, and for what group of stakeholders.

    i. Use of Library. Does anyone use it after school? Do you have hours when the school library is open after school? It is difficult to justify increased technology levels if your library only serves the school staff and pupils during regular school hours.

    j. Current Technology. What do you have (include numbers) and how it is used? You must be specific in how it is used. Just saying that students use technology for research is not sufficient.

3. Challenges (26–30). Included in the challenges section of the school library technology plan should be the technology vision for the school library. The technology vision is such an important part of the technology plan for several reasons. First, it provides a continual purpose for the library. Second, the vision statement should both challenge the library and invigorate it. This is the opportunity for the school librarian to look ahead, to get out of the day-to-day routine and see what technology can do for the library. This process is invigorating and should be a bit of a catharsis for the school librarian. Third, a vision statement should be a critical part of change. If we think back to the difference between movement and change discussed earlier, we can see the importance of change and should be able to visualize how the vision statement is part of the process. Fourth, if properly constructed, the vision statement can have a positive effect on the staff of the school library. The invigoration should carry over to the staff as they are able to see the positives of a move forward with technology. Finally, the vision statement is the standard against which progress with technology in the school library will be measured.

    When assessing challenges, one of the methods is a SWOT analysis. This is a common technique often used in the strategic planning process, but it is effective when assessing technology in the school library. What does SWOT stand for? Strengths, Weaknesses, Opportunity, and Threats.

    Once the SWOT analysis has been completed, the school library will then want to complete an examination of external factors that will affect the school library. Among these external factors are the following:

    a. Technology: A close look at the effect different types of technology can have on the school library is called for here.

    b. Economy: The state of the economy is a big factor when planning for technology in the school library. It is crucial you consider this and the impact the cost of technology will have on both the library's and the school district's budget.

    c. Markets: Do you know who your audience for services is? Does the technology positively affect them?

    d. Politics: We hate to have this as an external factor, but the power of politics is inevitable. The school librarian must be very circumspect when approaching those in the political arena.

    e. Law: Will any change of any local, state, or federal law affect the operation of the school library? What about the school code?

    f. Ethics: Ethical issues might include such things as copyright law or the use of filters for the Internet in the school library.

    g. Society: Are there societal forces that may come into play that will affect the procurement or use of different technologies in the school library?

4. Emerging Technologies (41–52). The section in the school library technology plan dealing with emerging technologies is at once both easy and difficult to construct. It is easy in that the section allows the school librarian to look into the future and try to figure what new technologies could be useful for the school library. The difficult part comes when the librarian attempts to predict what new technology will be useful. There is a big difference between could and will, and it is the job of the school librarian to attempt to discern the difference. Looking at emerging technologies is an area in which the technology coordinator and the IT staff can be of great assistance. They often have a better feeling for the new technologies.

5. Current Technology Environment (53–64). Assessing the current technology environment in the school library gives the school librarian the opportunity to see what is good and what is bad with relation to technology in the library. When you are assessing the current technology, the following are some factors to consider:

    a. Physical Environment. This was discussed in some detail earlier in the chapter, but it is an integral part of the technology plan itself.

    b. Network Infrastructure. This would include the wiring and the server capacity. A schematic of the network topology would be helpful.

    c. Network: In this area you will be discussing how reliable the network is and how fast it responds with different levels of network traffic.

d. Computer Hardware and Software: Servers. A table can be beneficial when describing the servers and server software serving the school library.

e. Computer Hardware and Software and Student and Staff Workstations. Remember that you are describing the technology environment at this point, not evaluating it.

f. Library Information System Software. This should be a detailed description of your OPAC.

g. Library-Wide Software Applications. In a school library this category might be very brief but should describe software used throughout the library to assist in the management of the library.

h. Desktop Software Applications. This description should include the productivity software used, the Internet browser, and the anti-virus software.

i. Technical Support. This should be a detailed description about how the school library gets its technical support. Typically this will be your IT department, but there may be better ways of obtaining it.

j. Data: Backups and Virus Protection. Both of these things are key and if you are not doing them or do not know how they are done you should.

k. Staff Skills: What is the level of your staff's technology skills? And, oh yes, what are yours?

6. Web Site Evaluation (83–98). Had we been discussing school library technology plans ten years ago, there would have been no need to discuss the school library's Web site. Today it is a necessity. Three stages must be discussed when looking at the school library Web site. Every school library needs to have a Web presence in order to deliver electronic resources to its users. The second stage is the creation of a digital library. This concept will be discussed in detail later in the book. The third stage is the ability of users to personalize the Web site for their own use. A school library Web site can have all three stages and still be ineffective if the creator did not pay close attention to some Web site design issues.

a. Why was the site created? This should be obvious to the user, but sometimes Web page creators are so concerned about the bells and whistles they forget the basics.

b. What is the library's goal with the Web site? Again, the obvious answer is to find information, but if the steps to do this are not clear, then some reevaluation may be in order.

c. Is it obvious to users what the library wants them to accomplish? This is closely related to (b), above.

d. What keeps the user at the site? Is it easy to do things and find information? Is there a lot of scrolling involved? Does it load quickly? All things to consider.

e. Why would a user want to return to the school library Web site? Again the obvious answer is they find the things they need, but ease of navigation and a visually pleasing site are important.

7. When we are evaluating the school library's Web site there are also a number of usability factors to take into consideration:

a. The graphics used should neither help nor hurt the site. Beware of large graphics, particularly if large numbers of your students still use dial-up connections.

b. Place text links on the page. Remember not all of your students will want to read a lot of text.

c. The navigation on the site and the content should be inseparable. Students (and teachers) are impatient. Make the navigation easy for them.

d. Links to Internet search engines are prominent and near the top of the Web page for ease of use. Searching and surfing are different.

e. Locally developed information should be found on your school library Web page. These are factors that will encourage users to return to the page.

f. Your Web page should be easy to find and well organized. Do not bury the link to the school library Web page deep on the school's Web page. It should be at the top of the page and highlighted.

g. The most general type of information descends to the most specific.

h. Each Web page in the Web site should be able to stand on its own. The index page should be just that, a page directing users to more information.

i. Students are impatient. Quick loading speed of the page is essential.

j. The Web page should be current. All links should be checked and updated frequently to avoid link rot.

k. The same standards or authority for information are used on the Web page as you do for the purchase of other library materials.

l. Links to multimedia require two things on the Web page. First, you should warn users that helper applications may be required, and second, provide a link so users can easily download the helper applications.

8. Recommendations (99–109). This is the section that will bring the whole plan together. This is where you recommend what technology you want for the school library, a plan for getting and using it, and

the cost of the technology. You may want to structure this part of the plan with the following continuum:

- Action Step: Timeline: Responsible Person
- Constructing the recommendations or for the breakdown of what should be recommended in the technology plan has no hard and fast rules. One author (Determining Your Technology Needs) suggested a breakdown as follows:
  - 40 percent hardware
  - 20 percent software
  - 20 percent professional development
  - 20 percent upgrades and future technology.

9. Plan Review and Update (111–118). The plan review and update is an integral part of the school library technology planning process. A technology plan should be a dynamic, not a static document. When the plan is adopted there should be a schedule for regular review and updating of it. Technology changes—so should the technology plan.

## FUNDING TECHNOLOGY AND TECHNOLOGY PLANS

### *General*

Funding for technology has always been an iffy situation. Because technology has only become so important in the past ten years, many school libraries and school districts have had to adjust their budget categories to account for the procurement of technology, and technology can become very expensive very quickly.

In an ideal situation the school district or the library will have a budget category for technology that is funded each year. It may be divided into several different subcategories, such has hardware, software, or networking, but the point is that there is a constant budget category for technology. The important thing to keep in mind is the technology budget category for the school library should be part of the library's discrete budget, not the technology department's budget or a curriculum budget.

At times, because of the high cost of technology, school districts have issued bonds to cover the cost of procuring technology. This can be effective, but the corollary is that once the bond money is gone there is often no money left to sustain technology. If your district uses bonded indebtedness for the procurement of technology, be sure that they are also willing to include the budget item for technology as discussed above. The funding of the technology plan will be the biggest challenge you will face in the entire process. All our technology plans will go for naught if there is no process in place to fund it. The funding issue is one that should be discussed and negotiated with the administration, in particular the business manager.

### Nontraditional Funding Ideas

Williams (2004, 212–215) discussed several nontraditional funding sources for technology. This is a somewhat new concept for many school librarians, but anyone who has conducted book fairs to raise funds for their library should be familiar with some of these nontraditional funding sources.

- Grants. We will discuss grants in some detail in the next section, including the elements that generally make up a successful grant proposal.
- Companies. Contact companies in your area that have even a tangential association with technology. They may be willing to either give funds or pieces of technology. Many of the larger concerns, such as Wal-Mart and Sony have been particularly willing to do this. Don't forget to contact companies that employ your school district's graduates.
- Publish and sell a book to raise funds for technology. This is really easier than it sounds. Many organizations self-publish items such as cookbooks as fundraisers. It may take a lot of legwork and coordination, but it can yield good returns.
- Update your technology plan. You ask, how is this a nontraditional funding source? By updating your technology plan you can add new and updated technology to it and then go to your school board to ask for funding. Again, remember to tie it to the curriculum.
- Beta test software. Many educational software companies are looking for sites to beta test their products. When you become one of them, the company will give you beta releases of the software to test. They often provide you with the final version when it is released.

### Grants

Many school librarians forget about grants as a funding source for technology because we think of ourselves as funded through taxation. Furthermore, many school librarians are not comfortable preparing grant applications because they have no experience doing so. Forget these preconceived ideas. Forget that your school district does not have a grant writer. Go to your state department of education's Web site and see what grant opportunities are available. Talk to local foundations to see if any of their grant categories could be used for school technology funding. It may surprise you, but many local charitable institutions may fit your needs and they are generally willing to keep funds in the community. If you do have a grant writer in your district, more the better, but they are generally administrative positions and disappear when budgets become tight.

Getting grants can be a bit of a complicated process. It certainly is more than calling the charitable institution and just asking for money. There is often a giving schedule, and, with the larger institutions, a request for proposal (RFP) process. The proposal submission process can include the following elements:

- A statement of the problem (or need) and a needs assessment. Remember the needs assessment you prepared for the technology plan? It can be reused here.
- Methodology. The methodology should clearly state how the requested money will help fulfill your library's mission and objectives. Be clear here. Do not use educational jargon. You are not necessarily dealing with educators, so they might not understand complicated "education speak."
- Plan of Operation. This would be where you would describe the design of the project, what you want, and how it will be used. A hint here would be to address the community in some way. Charitable institutions like to see multiple users of their money. For example, if you are asking for funds for computers, include a plan for the community to use them.
- Evaluation. This is a key to a grant proposal as it is to your technology plan. How will you measure success? Be sure to spell this out clearly and in measurable terms.
- Key Personnel. Who will make the grant work? Who will administer the money? Foundations will want names, not titles.
- Adequacy of Resources. Have you asked for enough funding to do what you say you want to do? If the agency likes your plan they will want to give you the money you need. Do not treat the budget request as if the funds are coming out of your own pocket.
- Impact. What will the impact of their funds be? Will it improve learning? How? Will it improve reading score? By how much? These are impact things foundations can relate to.
- Organizational Capability. Can your library support the resources? It is counterproductive to ask for forty computers when your library only has room for twenty or is not wired to network forty computers.
- Budget. The more specific the budget is, the more likely the project will be funded. Do your research and keep the budget up-to-date.

## ROLE OF THE SCHOOL DISTRICT TECHNOLOGY COORDINATOR

A question that I often ask in class is "Who is your best friend in the school district with relation to technology?" If the school librarian's answer is anyone other than the district's technology coordinator, they may want to reconsider their relationship to technology. In fact, whether you call him the IT director, the technology coordinator, or the network manager, he or she should be your best friend. The school district technology coordinator is responsible for all facets of technology in the school district—if you are that person's best friend, someone they can depend on, your library will be at the top of the list for their services.

Conversely, if you are always whining and asking for help for things you could easily do yourself, your school library will slip to the bottom of their priority list. Be self-sufficient. Help your technology coordinator; make him or her your best friend.

In Chapter 4 we discussed technology planning, the key for getting the right technology for the school library at the right time. In the introduction it was mentioned that technology planning might be so obvious that it does not need to be done. The material presented here should end ideas like that. If the school librarian is to get the technology he or she needs there must be a clear plan that ties technology to student achievement. Student achievement is what gets the attention of the administration and school board and gets the money required. In Chapter 5, copyright, censorship, filtering, and security will be discussed. These are disparate topics but fall into the broad category of issues with technology that can vex and frustrate the school librarian.

# RESOURCES

Anderson, Larry S., and John F. Perry, Jr. "Technology Planning: Recipe for Success." National Center for Technology Planning. 1994

Burke, John J.. *Neal-Schuman Library Technology Companion: A Basic Guide for Library Staff*. New York: Neal-Schuman, 2004.

Cohn, John M., Ann L. Kelsey, and Keith Michael Fields. *Planning for Integrated Systems and Technologies: A How-To-Do-It Manual for Librarians*. New York: Neal-Schuman, 2001.

"Determining Your Technology Needs." Forum Unified Education Technology Suite. http://nces.ed.gov/pubs2005/tech_suite/part_2.asp (accessed March 16, 2009).

Doggett, Sandra L. *Beyond the Book: Technology Integration into the Secondary School Library Media Curriculum*. Englewood, CO: Libraries Unlimited, 2000.

Gordon, Rachel Singer. *The Accidental Systems Librarian*. Medford, NJ: Information Today, 2003.

Ingersoll, Patricia, and John Culshaw. *Managing Information Technology*. Westport, CT: Libraries Unlimited, 2004.

Jurkowski, Odin L. *Technology and the School Library: A Comprehensive Guide for Media Specialists and Other Educators*. Lanham, MD: Scarecrow, 2006.

Matthews, Joseph R. *Technology Planning: Preparing and Updating a Library Technology Plan*. Westport, CT: Libraries Unlimited, 2004.

"Planning Your Technology Initiatives." Forum Unified Education Technology Suite. http://nces.ed.gov/pubs2005/tech_suite/part_1.asp (accessed March 16, 2009).

See, John. "Developing Effective Technology Plans. Minnesota Department of Education. http://www.nctp.com/john.see.html (accessed July 20, 2009).

Sibley, Peter H. R., and Chip Kimball. "Technology Planning: the Good, the Bad, and the Ugly." EDmin Library. http://edmin.com/news/library/index.cfm?function= showLibraryDetail&library_id=16 (accessed March 16, 2009).

Wesley, Ted. "Perceived Educational Technology Needs Survey." NCTP. www.nctp.com (accessed March 16 2009).

Williams, Brad. *We're Getting Wired, We're Going Mobile, What's Next? Fresh Ideas for Educational Technology Planning*. Eugene, OR: ISTE, 2004.

"Writing a Library Technology Plan: Assistance for New Hampshire Libraries." New Hampshire State Library. http://www.nh.gov/nhsl/electronic/e_rate.html (accessed July 20, 2009).

## QUESTIONS FOR RESEARCH AND DISCUSSION

1. Funding for technology in the school library is often difficult to obtain from local tax sources. Research the grants available for school library technology in your state and prepare a presentation that could be used for your school board to describe these sources and how the funds would be used for technology. It is important for your school board to understand how the technology will help the students, not just the school library as a whole.

2. In this chapter there were some lists of good things and bad things about technology plans. Either from the school that you currently work in or at a school nearby, obtain their technology plan and analyze against the guidelines given in this chapter. Prepare a report for the class detailing your findings.

3. Select a school district in your area. It can be the school district you work in, the school district where you will be student teaching, or the school district you reside in. Your task is to prepare a technology plan for the school libraries in the school district. It should follow the guidelines indicated in the chapter and should include a presentation for the class.

# 5

# *Copyright, Plagiarism, Internet Filtering, and Security Systems*

The four topics in this chapter may seem somewhat dissimilar to the casual reader, but they all deal with technology issues to a greater or lesser degree and are issues that can cause nothing but headaches for the school librarian. Copyright can affect technology and the school librarian in such areas as photocopying, copying software, and the fair use doctrine. Internet filtering has been a controversial topic as long as the Internet has been used in schools. While the American Library Association has a firm antifiltering stand, numerous federal and state laws and regulations define the landscape on this issue. The issue of plagiarism has been the nemesis of both school librarians and teachers as long as the research paper has been around. Technology has changed the playing field for plagiarism, as you will see. The experience with library security systems was, for many veteran school librarians, their first experience with technology beyond audiovisual hardware and software. These are all key issues and the influx of technology has only magnified them.

## COPYRIGHT: INTRODUCTION

No other concept in the field of school librarianship is less understood than copyright. School law courses do not focus on it, and the copyright law itself is so complicated that it has become a specialty of its own. Many administrators interpret "fair use" as "fair game" to copy workbook pages, while teachers and school librarians believe that "fair use" applies to everything within the school and that copyright law does not really apply to them. In other cases school librarians put a copyright warning on their photo copier and feel they have done their job with relation to copyright. We have all heard the term "copyright police," and in reality they are the

U.S. Marshals. You do not want to be in violation of copyright law if they visit your school district.

We will approach copyright in two ways. First we will look at some common copyright issues, and then we will examine some specific questions dealing with copyright. Butter, in "Copyright for School Librarians," posed some questions about materials to be copied:

- Do you have permission from the copyright holder to copy? If the answer is yes, proceed. If it is no, you may not copy.
- Is the material in the public domain? If yes, you may copy. If no, you may not.
- Does the material fall under the fair use guidelines? If yes, you may copy. If no, you may not.

This describes copyright in a nutshell; three questions and if the answer is yes, you may copy. Perhaps this was simple enough in the days before wide technology proliferation in schools, but technology has created a whole Pandora's box of copyright issues. *Tech-Learning, the Resource for Education Technology Leaders* has prepared twenty scenarios that deal with copyright and teachers. This may not address all of the issues, but it should give you grounding in copyright as applied to technology.

- A CD-ROM the librarian needs for a class is damaged or broken. May an archival copy be made? Yes, but it should be done in the library. If the same thing happens to a teacher, the archiving should be done in the library.
- A single copy of a piece of software has been installed on a school server so students can access it throughout the school. Is this permissible? Yes, if it is only used by one student at a time.
- A site license for a piece of software is held for the school. A newer version of the software is released, but the school elects to buy only five copies of the updated software, not a full site license. Students soon discover that work created on the new version of the software cannot be opened in the old version. Is it within copyright law to install the new version of the software on all computers to insure backward compatibility? The answer is no. The five new versions of the software can only be installed on five computers.
- Computer proficiency is mandated by the state with no budget provided for software. Can schools buy what they can afford and copy the rest? A gray area; some would say yes and some no. Contact the solicitor in your district for his interpretation and GET IT IN WRITING.

- More students and computers are available than software for a class. Is it okay to make enough copies of the software for the entire class? No. You are restricted to the number of copies of the software a school owns.

- Students are creating Web pages and have downloaded a large amount of material from the Internet. Are they free to put the materials on Web pages posted on the Internet? They may, but material protected by copyright must have the permission of the copyright holder.

- Web sites containing copyrighted material may be posted to secure, password-protected Web sites. Yes, as long as the sites' security is monitored.

- Material, including films, that are downloaded and used in schools fall under fair use guidelines. Generally true, but close attention should be paid to what file sharing sites are used.

- Audio clips can be downloaded from MP3.com and used in student projects. Yes, because MP3.com pays for its archives, as does United Streaming Video.

- Music and clip art downloaded from file-sharing sites may be used by teachers and posted to the school Web site so others can use it. Material pulled from file-sharing sites can be used but not shared.

- Students edit themselves into a video. Yes, this is allowable.

- Can movies shown on commercial television be digitized for computer use? They can be digitized.

- Material that you have legally placed on your Web site is being used by another school. This is an example of fair use in action. If it is okay for you, it is okay for them.

- Students in the school's day care classes want to entertain the day care children using videos they have purchased. Not permitted. This is for entertainment and falls outside of fair use.

- The creation of video compilations is considered to be fair use. No, the creation of video compilations is not permitted under fair use.

- The use of machines to overcome copy protection of media is not a violation of copyright. A moot point as these machines are prohibited, but educators do have the right to use things that are blocked technologically.

- Digital images of streets and businesses may be posted online in Web projects. Generally yes, but some sites such as Disneyland may be considered to be copyrighted.

- Ethnic music from a commercial CD for a project is considered fair use. This depends on some length limitations.

- Production of a video yearbook using commercial music is okay under fair use. No. Yearbooks are not considered to be educational material.

- A multimedia CD was produced using material that was copied under fair use. May this CD be sold for profit this year? No, because this involves wider distribution of the material.

### Myths about Copyright

Many, many myths about copyright have almost become urban legends. The first of these is that educators can do almost anything they want with materials because fair use trumps copyright law for educators. This myth is as old as the hills and really not true as we look at fair use guidelines in the next section.

The second myth says all materials pass into the public domain after the same amount of time and are no longer protected by copyright. At one time this was perhaps so but is certainly not true today as shown below:

| Date of Work | Protected From | Term |
|---|---|---|
| Created January 1, 1978 or after | When published | Life of the author plus 70 years |
| Published before 1923 | In the public domain | None |
| Published between 1923 and 1963 | When published with notice | 28 years plus 67 renewal years |
| Published between 1964 and 1977 | When published with notice | Same as above |
| Created before January 1, 1978 but not published | January 1, 1978 | Life plus 70 years or December 31, 2002, whichever is greater |
| Created before January 1, 1978 but published between then and December 31, 2002 | January 1, 1978 | Life plus 70 years of December 31, 2047, whichever is greater |

Brad Templeton (10 Big Myths About Copyright Explained) has written widely about copyright and has posited several more important myths about copyright. The myths are widely held and the description of why they are myths is thought provoking.

1. Works that do not have the copyright symbol (©) are not copyrighted. This has not been true for the most part since 1989. You have to assume material is protected by copyright if it is published even if the copyright symbol is not present.
2. If a copier does not charge for material there is no copyright violation. Not true; it is a violation, and damages could be assessed.

3. Usenet materials are always in the public domain. False, nothing is in the public domain unless it meets the description above or the creator explicitly gives up copyright ownership.

4. Defending postings as fair use. It may be true, but fair use is relatively complicated and restrictive.

5. If you do not defend copyright you lose it. False; you only lose copyright protection when you explicitly give it up. A recent claim by Google stating that anything out of print is in the public domain could change this.

6. Material you create based on another work belongs to you. False. These are what are called derivative works, and you must obtain the original author's permission. Of course this is not true if the original work is in the public domain. The many continuations of the Sherlock Homes stories would fall in this category.

7. Defendants' rights generally trump copyright law. Many people believed this right up to the time they were assessed damages for copyright violation in civil court.

8. Copyright violation is a civil matter, not a crime. Not true. As of the 1990s commercial copyright violation was made a felony (think losing your teaching certificate).

9. Copyright violation does not hurt anyone. From my standpoint this is absolutely false. Part of copyright law is the protection of the creative process. Using my creation for your use is harmful!

10. I received the copy via e-mail. No defense. Having a copy of something does not give you a copyright.

You see the myths. These are things many people believe about copyright but are not true. No wonder there are many lawyers whose specialty is copyright law.

## Fair Use

No concept of copyright law is more used but less understood than the fair use guidelines for teachers. As mentioned before, some educators use these guidelines as a carte blanche to do what they want; forget copyright laws. These are the ones who say "but I didn't know" when they are sued for copyright law violation. Unfortunately the fair use guidelines remind one of the Supreme Courts' discussions of pornography: "I can't define it but I will know it when I see it."

It is beyond my purpose in this book to spell out the specifics of the fair use guidelines. Many good sources for this information are available, such as *Technology and Learning's* "Copyright and Fair Use Guidelines for Teachers." Before looking at factors that could be considered a fair use test, keep in mind copyright protection does not apply to the following list of items, and you are free to use them as you please:

- Compilations such as phone books
- Materials in the public domain
- Freeware (but not shareware)
- U.S. government works
- Facts
- Ideas, processes, methods, and systems described in copyrighted materials

The four-factor fair use test attempts to put some system to what is essentially educational anarchy. For each question the uses on the left would be fair use while those on the right would generally require permission. Remember though that this is not scientific certainty. Different people can interpret the same things differently.

**Factor 1: What is the character of the use?**

| | | |
|---|---|---|
| Nonprofit | Criticism | Commercial |
| Educational | Commentary | |
| Personal | News Reporting | |
| | Parody | |

**Factor 2: What is the nature of the work to be used?**

| | | |
|---|---|---|
| Fact | Mixture of fact and imaginative | Imaginative |
| Published | | Unpublished |

**Factor 3: How much of the work will your use?**

| | |
|---|---|
| Small amount | More than a small amount |

**Factor 4: If this kind of use were widespread what affect would it have on the market for the original or for permissions?**

| | | |
|---|---|---|
| Proposed use tipping toward fair use. | Original out of print or unavailable | Competes with the original |
| | No ready market for permission. | Avoids payment for permission in an established permissions market. |
| | Copyright owner not identifiable. | |

Before we leave this morass of conflicting information about fair use, remember there are fair use quizzes available on the Internet. Try giving one to your faculty and see the red faces! I will end this section with a few statements that should help the school librarian and their faculty with regard to fair use in the library and education setting.

- Books and Periodicals
  - Copying cannot be used to create or substitute for anthologies.
  - Copying from "consumable" works such as workbooks or exercises is forbidden no matter what the salesman says.
  - Copying is not a substitute for purchasing nor can the same teacher copy the same thing term after term.
- Television and Video
  - Television programs may be taped for in-class use under the fair use guidelines.
  - Only copy prerecorded tapes with the publisher's permission.
  - Student-teacher created tapes can be copied as time allows.
- Internet
  - Material may not be posted from another Web site without permission.
  - Material from the Internet may not be compiled into a new work.
  - Copyright material cannot be scanned for school use.
- Music
  - Music cannot be copied for performances.
  - Music cannot be copied to avoid purchase.
  - Copied music must include a copyright notice.

### Dealing with Copyright Issues and Creating a Copyright Policy

It is almost inevitable that the school librarian will have to deal with copyright issues, be it with print materials or with technology. As mentioned before, the school librarian is not the "copyright police," but it pays to have some plan in mind when dealing with these tough copyright issues.

Carrie Russell in her article "Stolen Words" strongly recommended that school librarians know how to deal with copyright issues by:

- Having a thorough knowledge of copyright law and not being hesitant to advise school staff members about it.
- Learning about changes to copyright law, in particular the DCMA.
- Be aware of the user's rights and take all steps to find legal ways to allow access.
- Promote and publicize fair use guidelines.
- Consider the source of the information protected by copyright.

One of the things you as a school librarian can do is to create a copyright policy. This policy should be approved by your school administration and also by your school board. This will not protect everyone in the district, but it can protect you and the district as a whole. A typical copyright policy might contain the following sections that address both print and technology issues.

- A statement or introduction indicating the school library's intention to comply with copyright law.
- A complete description, with examples of fair use in a school setting.
- The rights of publishers on Web sites on the Internet.
- Copyright law regarding Web site construction.
- How student work and digital archives will be handled.
- Link rights on Web pages.
- Copyright netiquette.
- A statement of liability, in effect saying those who violate the policy may be liable to prosecution.
- A user permission form.

### Digital Content

As we speed into the twenty-first century, it is inevitable that copyright issues dealing with technology and the Internet will increase. Since the proliferation of computers, the piracy of software is of great concern both to the industry and to educators. Two factors have gone a long way toward easing this issue. The first is the level of security placed on computer software, making it much more difficult to make unauthorized copies. The second factor involves successful lawsuits by software manufacturers against school districts. Nothing makes a school district pay attention like having to pay damages in a civil case.

Other issues remain, such as the use of computer software on school networks without the requisite site license, but the biggest issue could well be the use of copyright-protected material on school Web sites. While the old adage "why reinvent the wheel" is probably appropriate for Web sites, copying material from someone else's Web site is probably a violation of copyright law. Often when it is done, it is so brazen that the metatags remain on the page. This would be an obvious intentional violation of copyright and might require communication directly with the district superintendent, while less obvious violations can be dealt with by the Web master.

As stated, copyright law is somewhat vague with relation to the Internet, but two things are not vague. First, ideas and facts or links on Web pages are not protected by copyright. Second, once a Web site is saved to disk, it is protected by copyright. The entire issue of copyright on the Web is far from settled, as is witnessed by the controversy over Google's attempt to digitize large library collections. The search engine giant Google has sought to digitize the book collections of many large public and academic libraries for their users. For researchers this would be a huge benefit. The results for the copyright holder are less clear. What is fairly certain, however, is that the issue will be decided by the courts.

## PLAGIARISM AND THE WORLD WIDE WEB

Plagiarism, or the using of someone else's words or ideas without attribution, has been a problem in schools for as long as term or research papers have been assigned by teachers. In the days before the Web, plagiarism often involved copying passages of sources, passing off someone else's words or ideas as the writer's, or simply making up sources. Students at all levels, even through graduate school, have tended to treat plagiarism as hardly a crime, almost a game. It is almost as though teachers fell off the turnip truck as it passed the school and immediately began teaching, completely unaware of how students attempt to plagiarize.

The proliferation of the World Wide Web has changed the face of plagiarism entirely and, in some ways, made the job of the school librarian much more difficult. First, students often think anything they find on the Internet is free and they can claim it as their own in a paper. This is a widely held belief not just among students but among adults; witness the school board member who felt school libraries did not have to buy books because everything is available for free on the Internet.

Second, students have the ease of copying material from a Web site and then pasting the passage into a word processing document. This is just such a simple process—even the most technically inept student can use this technique. Copy and paste makes it easy to plagiarize someone else's words or ideas.

The third thing that changed the face of plagiarism is the rise of term paper repository sites such as schoolsucks.com. These sites have many disclaimers in which they deny their site encourages plagiarism, but the facts remain that the sites provide fully attributed papers either for free or custom papers for a fee.

These three factors make plagiarism one of the most troubling increases in academic dishonesty. The fact is, as stated before, students do not look at plagiarism as a crime or as unethical, but rather as a game, a matching of wits, they must play with teachers.

What can the school librarian do to help their students avoid plagiarism?

- When you discover plagiarism, try not to be totally confrontational. While some students may be committed to plagiarizing, many others do not even realize they are plagiarizing.

- Have plenty of examples of correctly cited sources and papers that acknowledge sources available for the students to look at and use.
- Let the students know you are aware of the term paper sites and you know about copying and pasting material from the Internet.
- Encourage or foster discussions about plagiarism: the ethics and the legality of it.
- Encourage English teachers to give specific writing assignments rather than general assignments. This makes it much more difficult to find papers at the term paper repository sites.
- If a teacher comes to you with a paper you suspect is plagiarized, do not hesitate to use a search engine or a subscription service such as turnitin.com to test it.

These techniques are not foolproof, but they can make the process of recognizing plagiarism easier. They will not make students stop plagiarizing but perhaps they will think twice about it.

## FILTERING SOFTWARE

### *Introduction*

Early in the days of the Internet students discovered there was a whole lot of material out there that neither their parents nor their teachers would approve their accessing. In many cases the material was sexual in nature, but in other cases it was hate sites or sites that encouraged them to use their parent's credit cards. In those early days, we as school librarians were naïve enough to believe if our students accessed inappropriate material on the Internet, it would be okay if we took action against individual offenders rather than against all students. Were we wrong! Many school districts took action either as individual districts or as a part of an educational consortium to filter Internet content in the schools.

As the Internet continued to grow to the current size with an estimated 8 billion Web pages, the pressure grew to try to control what school library users were able to view on the Internet. The American Library Association stated that filtering the Internet was a violation of users' First Amendment rights. This was upheld in 1997 by the United States Supreme Court. Later, however, the Children's Internet Protection Act (CIPA) stated in essence schools or libraries receiving federal assistance either for Internet access or grants under LSTA must have Internet filters in place. In 2003 the Supreme Court upheld CIPA by holding that mandatory Internet filtering does not violate the First Amendment. Further rulings have mandated Internet filters for schools and libraries receiving Erate funds. We are probably beyond a discussion of whether or not Internet content should be filtered. Unless there is some drastic change in parents' views or the political climate, Internet filters are a fact of life in many school districts.

### *Internet Filters and Their Function*

Internet filters function in one of two ways. They either block Web sites that have been reviewed or they block sites based on keyword searches. The first is more reliable because someone has actually seen the Web site, but the second is more common because they are much cheaper to use. The difficulty with keyword filtering is that it does not differentiate among valid and invalid uses of particular keywords. As an example, students can rarely access information about breast cancer because the word "breast" is on the proscribed list.

The four basic types of Internet filters include client-side, content, server-side, and search engine. The first is client-side filters, which are installed as software on a computer and can be customized to meet the needs of the individual computer. It takes a password to disable the filter. This is the ideal filter for a small number of computers but becomes more unwieldy as the number of computers increases.

Content providers only allow their clients access to a portion of the Internet. The content they provide is monitored, and portions of the content may be added or deleted as the circumstances change. This type of filter is rarely used in library or school environments.

Server-side filters are very common in school districts. Everyone within the school district is subject to the filtering although certain people within the district may be able to bypass the filtering. This is particularly effective in school districts because you can set different levels of filtering for different areas in the school district. The filtering can be provided by the school district's ISP or by the district's technology staff.

Search engine filters are rarely used by school districts, but they are sometimes used by home computer users. Search engine filters are offered by search engines such as Google to filter out inappropriate links from search results.

There are several things filtering software can do:

- Restrict access to educationally valuable Web sites containing proscribed terms as mentioned above.
- Create issues for school librarians trying to teach responsible Internet use.
- Promote a political viewpoint.

There are a surprising number of things Internet filtering software cannot do.

1. Block all objectionable materials.
2. Block controversial materials.

3. Evaluate information on the Internet.
4. Take the place of the school librarian in student supervision.
5. Evaluate the age appropriateness of the Web sites.

Nearly fifteen years ago *From Now On*, an online education technology journal, listed a dozen reasons why filtering is not effective in schools. Those "reasons" are as valid today as they were then.

- They are not very effective. It is estimated only about 70 percent of material considered objectionable is actually filtered.
- They may work too well. This issue was discussed previously with the use of keyword filters.
- Kids are kids. The challenge of beating the filtering software is irresistible to children.
- The costs are often excessive.
- They can create false security. As noted above filters are only about 70 percent effective.
- Liability may be increased. If students access objectionable material, parents may feel compelled to sue.
- They may violate family values.
- They may violate community values. Often filtering software is more conservative than most communities.
- They may violate civil liberties. Court opinion currently rests with Internet filters, but that is always subject to change.
- They may define obscenity too narrowly.
- There are better ways to protect children than through the use of Internet filters.
- Children are capable of thinking (filtering) for themselves.

### Alternatives to Filtering Systems

If you are in a district that does not filter, two alternatives should be considered in planning for student use of the Internet. The first is having a viable acceptable use policy. This policy should define Internet and network use and should be signed by parents. Updating must be done on a regular basis. The second is to supervise students closely. As mentioned before kids will be kids, and you must supervise them. The encouraging of responsible student use of the Internet can also help alleviate the need for Internet content filtering.

## LIBRARY SECURITY SYSTEMS

More than 30 years ago when I began my school library career, other than the ever-present film projectors, the only technology the library had was a library security system. Several years before my arrival, the library was losing over $4,000 per year in library materials. This was in a high school of nearly 3,000 students with controlled access to the library. The year after a library security system was installed losses were less than $100. This is in keeping with research that shows school libraries lose 2–7 percent of a school library's collection annually. Prior to my first experience with a library security system in high school, my experience with a library security system was in the library at the University of Pittsburgh.

## Types of Security Systems

Two types of library security systems are manufactured, and three major vendors produce them. If your school library does not have a security system and you are losing substantial amounts of your collection, you may want to consider a security system. This is an area in which doing research and visiting other school libraries can help make your case to both your administration and to your school board. Also, your board may actually not object greatly to a onetime expenditure if it saves money over the long term. When you visit other schools make sure you view ones with both 3M security systems and Checkpoint systems. These are the major vendors, and you can find reviews of both types of systems in *Library Technology Reports*.

The major types of library security systems are "pass around" systems and "desensitizing" systems. Pass around systems, also known as radio frequency or radio frequency ID systems, are less expensive than desensitizing systems. Inserts, called CPs, are placed in library materials, and they must be passed around the security system. If materials are carried through the system, rather than passed around, an alarm sounds and the gate locks. This occurs even if a piece of library material is checked out, hence the term pass around.

Desensitizing systems are also known as full circulation or electromagnetic systems. With this type of system a sort of electromagnetic strip is place in library materials. When they are checked out the material is desensitized and can then be carried through the security system without setting it off. These are more expensive but are considered to be more efficient.

Consideration is given to several items related to security systems. First, for a security system to be effective, there has to be controlled access to the library. If students can come and go through multiple entrances and exits, the security system will never be effective.

When a security system is installed you must begin with a deterrence phase. Explain to students what the security system is and why it is there. Be sure to explain it thoroughly to teachers who have always entered and left the library as they pleased and perhaps even borrowed things without checking them out. Put up signs asking for cooperation and reminding them about the security system. Also be very clear about the consequences for trying to defeat the security system and emphasize enforcement.

The second step in effectively using a library is to ensure detection is fairly applied. If the alarm sounds, do not accept protests that the person does not have library materials. Make the person present everything they are carrying and make them go through the system again. While there are occasional false alarms, they are very rare. Never permit students (or teachers for that matter) to circumvent the system when leaving the library.

The final step is your response to attempts to circumvent the security system. Violations must be met with firm, consistent consequences. Apply them without fail or the presence of the library security system will be minimized.

## *Advances in Library Security Systems*

Library security systems have evolved over the years, and there have been many advances. Among the advances are

- DVDs and CD-ROMs are protected.
- Portable systems are available so that security markers can easily be applied away from main work areas.
- Configuration software has been developed for flexible installation of security equipment that adjusts for the physical characteristics of a library.
- Security corridors are ADA compliant.
- Multiple corridors can be purchased that can match all door widths.
- Auxiliary equipment may be tied in to security systems.

Security systems typically reduce loss by about 80 percent. At that rate they should pay for themselves in about two years and preserve valuable library materials from loss.

Chapter 5 discussed in detail four areas relating to library technology. First was copyright. Copyright can be a difficult problem for school librarians, and the problems have increased with the proliferation of the Internet. The second topic was plagiarism. This constant game between teacher and student has become more common with the wide use of electronic sources and the ease of "cut and paste." Filtering of the Internet is still a controversial topic, but some federal and state laws have made the issue moot. Finally was a discussion of library security systems. For many school librarians, they were the first experience with technology.

In Chapter 6 we will examine one of the most common technology applications in the school library, the automated library catalog. It is more commonly now known as the Online Public Access Catalog (OPAC), but it remains at the core of technology in the school library.

# RESOURCES

Allison, L., and R Baxter. "Protecting Our Innocents." Monash University. http://www.csse
.edu.au/publications/1995/tr-cs95-224/1995.224.html (accessed May 27, 2009).

Bennison, Nancy, and Don Lee. "Library Security: Protecting Valuable School Resources."
*Media & Methods* 37.7 (Aug. 2001): 13. *MasterFILE Premier.* EBSCO. http://
search.ebscohost.com (accessed April 22, 2009).

Bilal, Dania. *Automating Media Centers and Small Libraries: A Microcomputer-Based
Approach.* Greenwood Village, CO: Libraries Unlimited, 2002.

Butler, R. P. *Copyright for Teachers and Librarians.* New York: Neal-Schuman, 2004.

Callister, T. A., Jr., and Nicholas C. Burbules. "Just Give it to me Straight: A Case Against
Filtering the Internet," *Phi Delta Kappan* 85, no. 9 (2004). http://www.pdkintl.org/
kappan/k0405cal.htm.

"Copyright and Fair Use Guidelines for Teachers." http://www.halldavidson.net/copyright-
chart.html (accessed April 22, 2009).

"Copyright Condensed." Heartland Area Education Agency 11. http://www.somers.k12
.ct.us/~dnorige/documents/copyright.pdf (accessed May 27, 2009).

Craver, K. *Creating Cyber Libraries: An Instructional Guide for School Library Media
Specialist.* Greenwood Village April 22, 2009: Libraries Unlimited, 2002.

Doggett, Sandra L. *Beyond the Book: Technology Integration into the Secondary School Library
Media Curriculum.* Englewood, CO:April 22, 2009: Libraries Unlimited, 2000.

"A Dozen Reason Why Schools Should Avoid Filtering." *From Now On: The Educational Technology Journal* (March-April 1996). http://fno.org/mar96/whynot.html
(accessed April 22, 2009).

"Educators Guide to Copyright and Fair Use." Tech Learning. http://www.techlearning
.com/db_area/archives/TL/2002/10/copyright_answers.html (accessed May 27,
2009).

Fair Use of Copyrighted Materials." University of Texas. http://www.utsystem.edu/OCG/
IntellectualProperty/copypol12.htm (accessed April 20, 2009).

"Filtering." NetSafeKids. http://www.nap.edu/netsafekids/pro_fm_filter.html (accessed
April 22, 2009).

Harris, Robert. "Anti-Plagiarism Strategies for Research Papers." http://www.virtualsalt
.com/antiplag.htm (accessed May 27, 2009)

"Information Access & Delivery: Internet Access & Filtering Issues." The School Library
Media Specialist. http://eduscapes.com/sms/access/filtering.html (accessed April
22, 2009).

"Laws Relating to Filtering, Blocking and Usage Policies in Schools and Libraries."
National Conference of State Legislatures. http://www.ncsl.org/programs/lis/cip/
filterlaws.htm (accessed April 22, 2009).

Leland, Bruce H. "Plagiarism and the Web." http://www.wiu.edu/users/mfbhl/wiu/
plagiarism.htm (accessed May 27, 2009).

Lesk, Michael. *Understanding Digital Libraries.* Boston, MA: Elsevier, 2005.

Logan, Debra Kay. "Imitation on the Web: Flattery, Fair Use, or Felony?" in *The Whole
School Library Handbook,* edited by Blanche Woolls and David V. Loertscher,
179–182. Chicago:, IL ALA, 2005.

Miner, Barbara. "Internet Filtering: Beware the Cyber Censors." Rethinking Schools. http://
www.rethinkingschools.org/archive/12_04/net.shtml (accessed May 27, 2009).

Murray, Corey. "Study: Overzealous Filters Hinder Research." eSchoolNews. http://www
.eschoolnews.com/news/top-news/index.cfm (accessed May 27, 2009).

Peterson, Christine. "Filtering Software: Regular or Decaf?" http://www.txla.org/pubs/tlj-1q97/filters.html (accessed April 22, 2009).

Renard, Lisa. "Cut and Paste 101: Plagiarism and the Net." *Educational Leadership* (December 1999–January 2000): 38–42.

Russell, Carrie. "Stolen Words: Copyright in a Nutshell" in *The Whole School Library Handbook*, edited by Blanche Woolls and David V. Loertscher, 347–349. Chicago, IL: ALA, 2005.

Starkman, Neal. "Do the (Copy)right Thing," *THE Journal* (March 2008). http://thejournal.com/the/prinarticle?id=22173.

Templeton, Brad. "10 Big Myths about Copyright Explained." http://www.templetons.com/brad/copymyths.html (accessed April 22, 2009).

"University Laboratory High School Library Copyright Guidelines." University Laboratory High School Library. http://www.uni.uiuc.edu/policies/copyright.php (accessed April 20, 2009).

"Use of Entertainment Videos for Family Night." http://beckercopyright.com/id13.html (accessed April 20, 2009).

"When Works Pass into the Public Domain." University of North Carolina. http://www.unc.edu/~unclng/public-d.thm (accessed April 20, 2009).

Wiebe, Todd J., "College Students, Plagiarism, and the Internet: The Role of Academic Librarians in Delivering Education and Awareness." MLA Forum. http://www.mlaforum.org/volumeV/article1.html (accessed May 27, 2009).

# QUESTIONS FOR RESEARCH AND DISCUSSION

1. You have noticed that both teachers and students in your school are either unaware of or ignore copyright law. After some discussion with the school administration they have charged you with developing a copyright policy for your school. Your assignment is to prepare a copyright policy that can be adopted by your school board. Be sure to include information about fair use and touch on digital copyright issues.

2. There are many differing opinions concerning the efficacy of Internet filtering software. Prepare a position paper that could be presented to your school administration enumerating the positive and negative points of such software and describe each. Arrive at a conclusion that supports your conclusion.

3. Online term paper repositories are rampant on the Internet. Explore three such sites and download a paper from each. Then use different techniques available to determine if papers are plagiarized to assess the site's efficiency. Write a two- to three-page paper summarizing your findings.

4. Your library has been losing over $2,000 a year in library materials. Your administration has charged you with investigating the possibility of acquiring and installing a library security system. Analyze the different systems available, analyze the requirements of your library, and prepare a detailed analysis of your research. You may want to consult different vendors' Web sites to help gather information.

# 6

# *Library Information Systems*

In the original plan for this book Chapter 6 was tentatively titled "OPACs." As I did more extensive research of the subject it was obvious that OPAC only covers one part of what has become known as library information systems. For many school librarians, the installation of an OPAC, first called the Online Public Access Catalog, and then called an Automated Catalog, in the early to mid-1980s was their first experience with technology in school libraries. Some college and university libraries of that era had automated circulation systems, but they were cumbersome and often unreliable.

When considering a library information system, it is valuable to describe it as a system of modules and functions and as a combination of hardware and software. In their original incantation, library information systems were only quasi networked. This means they were probably networked within the library, but in order for any of the modules to be used, a patron or librarian had to be using one of the computers within this very small local area network. One should keep in mind much of this innovation was pre-Internet, so home access to the system was not even on the radar screen.

As mentioned, some larger libraries already were using automated circulation systems, but these small local area network systems brought automation to school libraries. In some cases the impetus was the creation of a statewide database such as Access Pennsylvania. It was a requirement for membership then, and still is, in Access Pennsylvania that the library install a library information system. Then, as now, a limited number of vendors have systems available. Follett software, which purchased one of its major competitors, Sagebrush, in 2006, controls about 70 percent of the library information system sales to schools.

# WHAT MAKES UP A LIBRARY INFORMATION SYSTEM?

The three major modules for library information system have remained pretty much the same throughout the evolution of the library information system Other modules have been suggested, some for the better and some for the worse, but the "big three"—the catalog, cataloging, and circulation—remain. In addition, when planning for the implementation of a library information system, some extremely important issues must be considered.

- System Issues
  - Hardware Requirements. Does the system require state-of-the-art hardware or can older equipment be recycled for use? At one point it was probably practical to use older hardware, but if all computers are now used to access the system, then relatively powerful hardware will be required.
  - Support Agreements. School libraries using early versions of library information systems could live with support agreements that were not 24/7. That is no longer true as the systems are available from home, and user support is required on a 24/7 basis.
  - Training. Nothing is less useful than technology put in place for teachers and school librarians without appropriate training. This is a sure recipe for the failure of technology. See how the training is provided and if there is an add-on fee for training. Explore the possibility of online training. Determine if there is follow-up training as the product evolves.
  - Reports. This issue seems to be a bit incongruous here, but the report function of a library information system is where you will analyze data and produce information your administration and school board may find interesting. Your board spent a lot of money on a library information system. The reports you produce can help convince them they made a good investment.
  - Data Conversion. I have saved the knottiest problem for last: conversion of your card catalog into a machine readable format. This is also known as retrospective conversion. To accomplish this, the school library typically sends its shelf list off to a vendor who converts it. The costs for this procedure can be considerable, but most statewide initiatives such as Access Pennsylvania paid for retrospective conversion.

All librarians would love to report retrospective conversion produces a perfect catalog. Unfortunately this is far from true. If your collection had poor cataloging before conversion, it will now have poor automated cataloging. Some of these early statewide initiatives are still suffering the consequences of poor cataloging.

- Cataloging Module
  - Importing Records. An efficient library information system should allow for the importing of records both from jobbers and from one or more statewide catalogs. Further, users should be able to create complete, accurate MARC records within the cataloging module. The inclusion of local information into the record should be seamless.
  - Cataloging of Web Sites. As the procurement of information from the Web becomes more common, library information systems should have procedures for cataloging Web sites.
  - Merging Records from the Existing System. The issues accompanying retrospective conversion were discussed above. A further area of concern is data migration when the system is upgraded or replaced.
- Circulation Module
  - Security. Early in the progression of library information systems when they were, at best, small local networks, security was a major issue. It is still important but is generally handled on a level above the library. Just be sure you have an override password and you know how to use it.
  - Internal Calendar. Be sure that circulation periods are able to be tied to specific dates and holidays and weekends are automatically calculated into the system.
  - Import of Patron Records. Just as you should be able to easily import catalog records, it should be equally easy to import patron records. Every time a class moves to a new building or graduates from high school and a new one enters, you do not want to have to do the update manually. This may require some assistance from your technology coordinator.
  - Error Alerts. The system should have both audible error alerts and visible alerts. Both should not allow further work until cleared.
  - Check-out Blocks. If you block patrons from checking out materials when they have something overdue, you may wish to make certain you have an override for this.
- Catalog Module
  - Searching. Searching should be able to be done using subject orkeyword. Keywords should automatically be generated by the system.

- Truncation and Wild Card. Patrons should be able to use both truncation and wild cards so if they are not sure of a search term, they can still get results.
- Stop Words. This is not as major a problem as it once was, but it goes without saying that words such as "an" and "the" are treated as stop words.
- Auto Complete Spell Check. The catalog module should automatically correct the spelling of common words as well as those in error because of such things as keyboard transposition.
- Mouse or Keyboard Search. The system should search equally well either way.

These are the basic modules that should be part of any library management system. Other modules available in some systems that can greatly enhance the utility of your system include the following:

- Serials module. More and more school libraries are automating the processing of serials, and most of the new library information systems have this module.
- Acquisition module. Most modern school library information systems have an acquisitions management module included, as well as an interlibrary loan module.

As we move to single-search, visually oriented library information systems, there are several other modules that are almost requirements to provide the best search experience for your students. They all relate to providing all available resources using a single search. These modules include the following:

- Electronic Resource Management Systems. These are more for use by the staff than patrons, but they allow the management of magazine subscriptions with other electronic resources.
- Metasearch. This is the single search school librarians and students have always wanted. It allows a single search for books, periodical indexes, electronic databases, and the Internet, and it can be done from school or home.
- Digital Library Products. These modules allow libraries to manage all of the digital collection.

## HOW SCHOOLS ARE USING LIBRARY INFORMATION SYSTEMS

The obvious response to this heading is that school libraries are using library information systems as a catalog, for circulation, and for cataloging, but that would be a large oversimplification. A 2006 survey conducted by

Daniel Fuller, a faculty member at San Jose State University, showed trends that should be of concern to school librarians who are advocates of the best library service possible to their students.

First, most schools are using automation systems more than five years old. While 75 percent of school libraries had automated by 2002, Fuller found that less than one in five were using the latest version of the library information system. This is a direct reflection on the decline in school library budgets and is often the result of school districts redirecting funds to meet No Child Left Behind mandates. This situation has only been exacerbated by the 2008–2009 economic downturn.

Second, Fuller showed school librarians are very satisfied with the library information system they are using, even if it is not the latest and greatest. They find their systems stable and reliable and apparently have established a comfort level with their systems. In particular they are satisfied with the different modules of their systems. The librarians are most satisfied with the circulation module, followed by the cataloging module, the OPAC module, and then vendor support. While vendor support showed last here, 86 percent of the school librarians queried were either extremely likely or somewhat likely to use the same vendor and purchase the same system (Fuller).

Although school librarians appear to be very satisfied with their library information system, many are only scratching the surface of the system's capability. For example, a small (less than 50 percent) number of school librarians use their systems to print daily reports. With so many one-person school libraries, this is somewhat understandable, but it is discouraging that the power of the library information system is ignored.

## ADVANTAGES, DISADVANTAGES, AND POSSIBLE IMPROVEMENTS FOR LIBRARY INFORMATION SYSTEMS

Nearly every school library textbook published in the past ten years lists the advantages and disadvantages of library information systems. As time passes, the advantages become more numerous and the disadvantages far fewer. In the next three sections I will attempt to distill to one list of each, along with creating a list of some improvements that might be made to library information systems.

### *Advantages of Library Information Systems*

- Library information systems provide more search options for patrons than traditional card catalogs. Any piece of data in the MARC record can be searched by a modern library information system.

- Library information systems can encourage more school library use because of their ease of use.
- Automated library information systems present the school library as being "up" on technology.
- Library information systems allow remote access to the school library's resources.
- Modern library information systems allow single-query searching, not only allowing patrons to search the book collection but also integrating other electronic resources into the catalog.
- These systems simplify inventory procedure. The bane of all school libraries is made as easy as scanning bar codes.
- Routine tasks are made simpler, getting materials on the shelves more quickly.
- Library information systems reduce the cost of providing a catalog. While initial costs are high, sustaining costs are lower than such labor-intensive duties as typing and filing catalog cards. This does not even address a constant issue with traditional card catalogs: misfiled catalog cards.
- In addition to improved access to materials, library information systems also provide the check-out status of library materials. This advantage alone makes the system purchase worthwhile.
- Library information systems encourage collection development and resource sharing. Since time immemorial school libraries have been self-contained boxes with access only to their own collection. A library information system makes it easy to see the holdings of other school and public libraries to encourage resource sharing. Further, these days of reduced school library budgets make shared collection development a requirement, and a library information system can simplify the task.
- These systems make importing and exporting MARC records much simpler. This simplification can substantially improve the quality of school library cataloging.

These are eleven good reasons for installing library information systems in a school library. In reality, there is no school library that should not have one in place. With today's technology-rich atmosphere there should be a library information system in every school library.

### Disadvantages or Problems with Library Information Systems

All of the reasons given in the last section, along with the author's admonition that a library information system is crucial in today's school library, do not hide the fact there are some problems associated with library information systems. All of these problems can be overcome if the school librarian plans carefully and is dedicated to the goal of providing students with the best educational experience possible.

- Installation of a library information system can be time consuming. The entire planning process, from idea to procurement, can take time school librarians rarely think they have. This is particularly true in a school library with one school librarian and no clerical help. Furthermore, once the system is installed it must be maintained, and this again takes time away from other tasks.
- Library information systems can be costly. The multitude of costs associated with the successful implementation of a library information system cannot be overlooked, such as hardware, servers, furniture, consumable supplies, and other items. In addition, the retrospective conversion alone can be extremely expensive for the school unless, as with Access Pennsylvania, many of these costs are assumed by the state. This is an area ripe for grant writers, as many funding sources view library automation as a worthwhile use of grant money.
- The implementation of library information systems can take up so much time school librarians, particularly in small schools, may not have the time required to work with students or to take on new responsibilities. While library information systems can be labor saving, they can create new tasks that did not exist before.
- System downtime. In an ideal world no library information system would ever be down. The reality is systems do sometimes go down. It is not as common as it once was, but system downtime can be disastrous. Plan for it!
- At times there are levels of knowledge library information system users must possess in order to successfully use the system. These levels of knowledge do not build on each other but are discrete knowledge bits users must possess.
  - The first level of knowledge is a conceptual level of knowledge. This is knowledge of how to translate an information need into a search. At times it is a giant leap from searching for Shakespeare to searching for dramatizations of *The Taming of the Shrew*.
  - The second level of knowledge is a semantic level of knowledge. This takes the search to the formulation of a search query that returns only relevant results.
  - The final level of knowledge is the technical skill necessary to actually operate the library information system. It does little good to have a state-of-the-art library information system if the students do not know how to use a mouse or lack other necessary technical skills.

*How to Improve the Library Information System*

No system is ever perfect, the claims of vendors notwithstanding. However, a few common-sense simple steps can be taken to improve the school library information system.

- Database Improvements. This seems so simple as to be superfluous, but the reality is there is much poor cataloging in school libraries. Cataloging, particularly original cataloging, is often a low priority in school libraries. Sometimes working with the database a few minutes every day can make a huge difference in the quality of the database.
- Vendor Improvements. While improvements in library information systems sometimes seem to come too fast to deal with, the school librarians should carefully look at these improvements. Some you may be able to use, some you may not. Remember though, some vendor improvements may significantly improve your library information system.
- New Initiatives. Some of the same things discussed above also apply to new initiatives. Examine them carefully and select the ones having the biggest positive effect on your library information system.

## SELECTING A LIBRARY INFORMATION SYSTEM

It is time to move forward and evaluate library information systems for your school library. We will approach it in two ways. First, Burke (2006, 82–85) provided ten questions school librarians should ask about library information systems. Second, Doggett (2000, 110–111) provided a more detailed checklist of items school librarians should consider when evaluating library information systems.

*Questions to Ask*

- What is the size of the collection? Be sure the library information system is robust enough to handle the collection.
- How many users can the system accommodate? This is an absolutely critical question. If the system you are examining cannot handle all of your users, run, do not walk away from it.
- What modules are needed? Examine your needs closely and compare them to the module available in the system. While it is sometimes possible to add modules as time passes, it is often difficult to do it efficiently.
- How many remote users are anticipated? Remote users are those who use the system outside the walls of the school. This can be a deal breaker if your library information system does not provide remote access.
- How long will it take to convert from cards to MARC? Think vendors for retrospective conversion. This is their business and

although it can be pricey you have to go that route unless you have unlimited time.

- Should you weed before converting? Without a doubt. Be ruthless when you weed your collection. It can be painful but it will save you some serious money in your retrospective conversion.
- How simple is the migration to the new system? Your vendor and their technical support team have to be on site to ramrod the migration.
- Can the interface be modified? Inevitably you will not like parts of the interface. Can you change it and how difficult is it to make interface changes?
- Is the staff interface efficient and intuitive? If not, you might want to look in a different direction.
- What are the vendors' future plans? Imagine the surprise of those Sagebrush users when Follett bought them. Try to find out if the company is financially secure.

### Library Management System Vendor Checklist

- Cost
  - Are there volume discounts for an entire school district?
  - Can the system be phased in over a period of years to save money?
  - How does the cost compare with other vendors?
  - Are the costs consistent with the services available?
  - Is there a charge for updates?
  - Is there an annual subscription cost?
- Support Contracts
  - What are the fees for phone and online support?
  - How quickly does a vendor stop supporting a product when a new version is introduced?
  - Is there both toll-free and help desk support?
- Training
  - Does the vendor provide training to the school library staff?
  - Does the vendor assume responsibility for loading software?
- Z39.50 Compatible
  - Is the system compatible with Z39.50 conventions?
- Use
  - Is there an integral spell checker?
  - Is navigation intuitive?
  - Does it permit Boolean searching?
  - How long will it take to teach the system to students and teachers?
  - Is there an efficient on-screen help system?
  - Are closing routines simple?

- Recommendations
  - Have you surveyed other school libraries using the system to determine satisfaction?
  - What weaknesses have others found in the system?
  - Were some functions promised but not delivered?
- Capacity
  - Is the system compatible with your current computers and network?
  - Can the system handle all required transactions?
  - Can reports be run in the background without system degradation?
  - What are the systems patron and record capacity?
- Flexibility
  - Can the system grow?
  - Can the database migrate easily to a new vendor's product?
  - Can the system's interface be customized?
  - Can custom reports be created?
  - Are the systems compatible with those of all libraries in your district?
- Vendor Support
  - How long has the vendor been in business?
  - What enhancements to the system are planned?
  - Does the vendor update when new hardware is purchased?
  - Will the system function on both school and district-wide networks?

## THE FUTURE OF LIBRARY INFORMATION SYSTEMS

The future for library information systems includes the ongoing move to visual systems with single-search capability. With these systems patrons will be able to enter a research question on one screen and the return will be books from the collection, items from fee-based databases, and vetted Web sites. Further, students will have had instructions in query formulation, so they will be able to create efficient searches. Another area for the future of library information system is that of digital libraries. Those concepts will be discussed in Chapter 8. In Chapter 7 the focus will be on the library Web page and Web site, before we move to digital libraries in Chapter 8.

## RESOURCES

Bazirjian, Rosann. "The Administration and Management of Integrated Library Systems." *LRTS* 1 (2001). http://www.ala.org.

Bilal, Dania. *Automating Media Centers and Small Libraries: A Microcomputer-Based Approach*. Greenwood Village, CO: Libraries Unlimited, 2002.

Brisco, Shonda. "Technology Connection: Visual OPACs," *Library Media Connection* (November/December 2008): 56–57.

Burke, John J.. *Neal-Schuman Library Technology Companion: A Basic Guide for Library Staff*. New York: Neal-Schuman, 2004.

Cibbarelli, Pamela. "ILS Marketplace: School Libraries," *MultiMedia Schools* (September 2003). *MasterFILE Premier*. EBSCO. April 22, 2009 http://search.ebscohost.com.

Doggett, Sandra L. *Beyond the Book: Technology Integration into the Secondary School Library Media Curriculum*. Englewood, CO: Libraries Unlimited, 2000.

Everhart, Nancy. "How Relevant are Standardized Subject Heading to School Curricula," *Knowledge Quest* 33, no. 4 (2005). *MasterFILE Premier*. EBSCO. April 22, 2009. http://search.ebscohost.com.

Fiehn, Barbara. "Social Networking and your Library OPAC," *MultiMedia Schools* (September 2008). *MasterFILE Premier*. EBSCO. April 22, 2009 http://search.ebscohost.com.

Fuller, Daniel. "School Library Journal & San Jose State University 2006 Automation Survey," *School Library Journal* (October 1, 2006). http://www.schoollibraryjournal.com/.

Harris, Christopher. "Fishing for Information: The Next-Generation OPAC," *School Library Journal* (January 1, 2008). http://www.schoollibraryjournal.com/.

Jurkowski, Odin L. *Technology and the School Library: A Comprehensive Guide for Media Specialists and Other Educators*. Lanham, MD: Scarecrow, 2006.

Kochtanek, Thomas R., and Joseph R. Matthews. *Library Information Systems: From Library Automation to Distributed Information Access Solutions*. Westport, CT: Libraries Unlimited, 2002.

Murphy, Catherine. "The Online Catalog on the Way to the Millennium," *MultiMedia Schools* 5, no. 3 (1998). *MasterFILE Premier*. EBSCO. April 22, 2009 http://search.ebscohost.com.

"Next-Generation Flavor in Integrated Online Catalogs," *Library Technology Reports* (July–August 2007). http://www.techsource.ala.org.

Woolls, Blanche. *The School Library Media Manager*. Englewood, CO: Libraries Unlimited, 1994.

# QUESTIONS FOR RESEARCH AND DISCUSSION

1. Your library is considering either upgrading or changing its library information system. Using a combination of the criteria presented in this chapter, visit three other schools using different systems and compare their capability. Using this data prepare a recommendation to be presented to your administration and school board.

2. Prepare a presentation for your school board that traces the history of library management systems. Be sure the presentation includes graphics and shows the use and value of each of the modules in the library information system.

3. The interface a user uses helps the user determine how they react to the system. Examine two major library information systems to determine if the interface is user friendly. Suggest ways that the interface could be improved to make it more user friendly.

# 7

# *School Library Web Sites*

As school libraries move forward with technology, a question that arises is whether your school library needs a Web site or a Web presence. Our administrators, teachers, and students and even their parents are Internet savvy enough to know research is done on the Internet. For the most part their research consists of Googling a search term and using the first three or four sites listed as the basis of their research, regardless of the quality of the information returned by the search.

So how does searching behavior relate to a school library Web site? Easy—you want your primary audience, your students and teachers, to use your Web site as the place they go for credible, reliable, current information. According to Warlich, you want to help students become effective learners and to assist teachers in providing quality educational experiences (Warlich 2005). This all brings us full circle and answers the question, why have a Web site? When you have decided that your library needs a Web site, you should consider several things.

- What is the purpose of the Web site? If the purpose of the site is anything but education, you may want to rethink things.
- What do you want to accomplish with the Web site? We will examine stages in the evolution of Web sites later in this chapter.
- What should the Web site users be able to do? This depends a great deal on what stage the Web site is in.
- What will keep your users on your school library Web site? This question has no easy answers, but as you progress through the chapter you should get some ideas about this issue.
- What encourages a user to return to your Web site? See above.

## TOUGH QUESTIONS, MANY SUGGESTIONS

Let us think for a few minutes about the Web site you have now or the Web site you will be constructing. The evolution of a Web site begins with the question, why have one? The first stage of Web page development is the "why we are here" Web page. It is pretty basic and describes the library and what the library does. Schools with a minimal Web presence often have Web pages that fall in this category. The second stage is a user-centered digital library. At this stage students are able to do research and may, in fact, use the page as the starting point for all research. This is a very common stage in school library Web page development. Finally, and certainly still uncommon, is the school library Web page allowing user personalization. Most school libraries are far from this stage, but it is one that will establish you as a leader in the field.

We have addressed the "why" as it relates to school library Web pages. While we will address what should be on that web page in greater detail later, let us start with what an effective school library Web page should have, as a minimum,

- The ability to interact with the library's OPAC.
- A gateway to the library's electronic resources.
- Remote access to the library's databases.
- Library tutorials or how-tos.
- A virtual reference section.
- Access to library blogs (unless this is prohibited in your school).

## HOW TO CREATE THE SCHOOL LIBRARY WEB PAGE

In an ideal world the creation of Web pages and Web sites would be as easy as using a word processing program. It actually can use word-processed programs, but there are several caveats associated with this type of Web page creation. Let us go back in history a bit and look at early Web page creation. It was essentially a programming job done by computer programmers knowledgeable in hypertext markup language. (HTML). Many computer professionals would hold this is still the best way to create Web pages. Fortunately for the rest of us there are other ways to create Web pages.

If you are using Microsoft Office as your productivity software, each of the applications, Word, Excel, PowerPoint, and Access, will allow you to save your work as a Web page. Your response could well be "Why would I want to use anything else?" Two reasons explain why you probably do not want to use these as your Web creation software. First, these programs do not allow the creation of fully integrated Web sites. (Note here there is a difference between Web pages and Web sites. A Web site is generally a group of related and linked Web pages.) Second, using these programs does not give you the close control over content you will want to best showcase your school library.

The second way of creating pages and Web sites is by using Web creation software. The two leaders in this field are Microsoft Expression Web and Macromedia DreamWeaver. These are both relatively complex programs and not particularly intuitive. They both have the capability of producing professional, functional Web sites after some level of training. Check with your local two- or four-year school to see what training might be available in your area. Both of these programs will allow you to create individual Web pages or integrated Web sites.

If your creative juices are not flowing or you feel you just do not have the time to do a Web page justice, take a look at some of the Web page template services that are available, such as Schoolwires. These types of programs do not have a great deal of flexibility, but you can turn out an attractive product.

Now that you know how to do it, or at least what programs to use to do it, the next issue is how to get your Web page or Web site actually on the Internet. Generally your ISP (Internet service provider) will host your Web site as part of the services your district pays for. If your district is its own ISP, then it follows that the district will host your Web site. In the highly unlikely event that the ISP that the school district uses does not host Web pages, it is likely that another commercial ISP (Comcast, etc.) will provide a certain amount of server space to host Web pages.

The next issue you have to deal with is how to get your school library Web site from your computer to your ISP's Internet server. This step can get very technical very quickly, so unless your Technology Coordinator is going to do it, you need a bit of technical expertise. The simplest way to upload Web sites to an Internet server is to use a file transfer program (FTP) program such as Filezilla or Cute FTP. The FTP allows you to post your Web site to your ISP relatively quickly and easily. If you are not sure about uploading your Web site, your Technology Coordinator should be your next stop.

## WEB DESIGN

Many books written discuss effective Web design. Our purpose here is not to be all inclusive because those books are available, but rather to give you some basic guidelines to make your Web side attractive and user friendly.

In 2006, Jennifer L. Wholleb (May 2006) provided guidelines to school administrators about considerations they should make when designing a district Web site. While this is a higher level than a school library Web page, it gives a good insight into what administrators think is important in Web site design.

- Be sure your Web site is professional, attractive, and informative. It is the first place you can make an impression online when people want to find out abut the school district or your school library.
- Make sure the most basic information people would want about the school district is easy to find. This would include telephone and fax numbers, street addresses, and e-mail addresses. It is nice to talk about great test scores, but make the basic information easy to find.
- The school's mission statement should not be the first thing you see on a Web page. While the mission is important and should be readily available, if it is the first thing you see, you have to consider if the mission of the page is to promote the mission or the school.
- Do not, under any circumstances, use generic, educational clipart! It is too cutesy. Also, avoid those stock photographs of the school.
- Keep your Web site easy to read and use. Complicated photos and graphics, music, and streaming video are all nice things to have, but keep in mind some of your users may be still using dial-up connections.
- Keep your Web site up to date. Always have the last update date on the page. Out-of-date information and invalid links are worse than no information at all. This is one of the main reasons maintaining a Web site cannot be one of those "do it when you have time things." There is never time!
- Use standard fonts. Specialty fonts look unprofessional and can be extremely hard to read.
- Do not make your Web site too busy. Remember less is more and content can be buried in cuteness.
- Do not use "under construction" pages on the Web site. Do not put a page on the site until there is content on it.
- Updating the Web page. Fix broken links when updating the Web page. Either correct the link or eliminate it. Your credibility is at stake.
- Forget the artsy introduction page. Get to the point.
- You can never test the Web site too much. Test it with different browsers and on a dial-up connection.

## WEB PAGE DESIGN

What do you want your school library Web site to look like? A simple answer is it should be attractive and draw users back to the Web site. At the same time it should be informative and easy to use. This just scratches the surface of design, and design issues that must be considered. On one hand you want to think like a librarian. You know what your patrons need on a Web page and what they will use. On the other hand you also have to think like a Web designer. That is difficult for most school librarians because they are not really Web designers. Your Web designer role must take over and determine what can be done within what your patrons want.

Of prime importance in Web design are issues of accessibility and usability. Having accessible Web pages means people with disabilities can use all parts of your Web page. Anything on a Web page that is an image or words (and that is almost everything) must be considered for accessibility. When you are constructing your school library Web site, consider the following about images:

- Images can take considerable time to download. This is especially true if your students are using dial-up connections.
- Images can take an inordinate amount of time to create and can be difficult to change.
- Text in an image cannot be changed to allow easier reading.
- Text from an image cannot be copied and pasted.

When you are working with your Web page there are some rules with relation to images and accessibility you may want to consider.

1. Always include an .alt attribute with a description of the content when your image has information.
2. Always include a "long description" attribute if the image has a large amount of information associated with it.
3. Make images as small as practicable to speed downloading.
4. Rarely use image maps, and when you do, have a good reason for doing that.
5. Do not rely on color to mark things on the Web page. This has color blindness issues.
6. Make sure your Web page does not do unexpected things like open in a new window unless there is some indication of what will happen.
7. Make your default font and font size readable.

Usability is how well your students can use the Web site to do what they want it to do. A few basic rules you can follow in order to assure your site is usable include the following:

1. Consider what your audience (read students) need.
2. Make sure your Web site is well organized so users can easily find what they want.
3. If your site is well organized then insure the site is easy to navigate.

4. Be sure the content on all Web pages is clear, well organized, and well written.

The next few sections in this chapter will address design issues considered by all school librarians when they are working at creating their Web site. Matthews (2004, 88) has created what he calls ten rules of good design:

1. Every page must have content and it must be easy to read.
2. The first color on any Web site should be white. White is a great background color and can take almost any dark color font.
3. The second color on any Website is always black. See the comments for (2).
4. The third color is red or . . .
5. Never letter space lowercase fonts.
6. Never, never use all caps. It does not emphasize and is really hard to read.
7. The cover of a Web page should be a poster.
8. Never use more than one or two typefaces on a Web site.
9. Make things as large as possible on a Web site.
10. While consistency on a Web site is good, it has to be broken up occasionally.

Kochtanek and Matthews (2002, 192–193) described some Web page design guidelines that piggyback on the ideas noted above. The authors broke these into visual considerations and practical considerations.

### Visual Considerations

- Never use all caps for emphasis.
- Insure links are in prose or definition lists.
- Break up your content. Page after page of text is boring.
- Only one or two fonts per Web site.
- Use white space effectively.

### Practical Considerations

- Never use more than three images per page. Think of the poor user with a dial-up connection.
- Neither clash nor blend together the background and text on a Web page.
- Use light background colors. White is always good!
- Use no more than four colors per screen.

These lists have given some very specific suggestions concerning Web site design. We probably could distill these down to a few items.

- The graphic design of a Web site will neither help nor hurt the Web site.
- Text links are absolutely vital. Try your best to avoid using images as links.
- The content and navigation of a Web site are inseparable.
- All Web sites must have a search engine link.
- No matter what else is true, a Web site must be good to be used.

## WEB SITE DESIGN ERRORS; OR, UGH, WHAT AN UGLY SITE

This section is the list to end all lists, but there are so many bad Web pages that every use of the items listed here should be etched in every school librarian's mind. All anyone has to do is surf the Web for a while to see what is bad, and there is plenty of it. You might call this list "don't do this or you will have an ugly Web page."

- Do not use frames. Web pages using frames are nothing but trouble for users. They often display incorrectly and can be almost impossible to print. Fortunately, new Web design programs like Microsoft Expression Web have effectively eliminated the use of frames.
- Do not use bleeding-edge technology. Pay attention to the fact that most of your students don't have the newest technology—don't use it just because it is cool.
- Do not use scrolling marquees and animations. All they do is slow page loading down and distract the user from the real mission of the Web site.
- Do not use complex URLs. While it is always desirable to go directly to the location of information, sometimes you want to back off a screen or two to simplify the URL link.
- Do not use orphan pages. Orphan pages are those that do not contain any identifying information and do not provide navigation back to the previous Web page.
- Do not use long, scrolling pages. Scrolling pages are deadly, deadly, deadly! Most Internet users, both adults and children, will stop scrolling after about two pages.
- Do not forget your navigation bar, site search, or site map. It is never good for your users to have to guess where they are on your Web site.
- Do not use nonstandard link colors. Your users with color blindness issues will be completely lost on the Web site.

- Do not use old information. Of all the issues we discuss, dated information will cause your Web site to lose credibility more quickly than anything else.
- Do not have long download times. This is a direct result of a large number of big images.
- Do not use distracting splash pages. Of particular note are glitzy introduction pages. Skip it and get right to the content.
- Do not use unnecessary design items. As we mentioned previously, they distract from the ease of use of the Web site.
- Do not use the same Web design for the school's intranet. Doing this can create a lot of unnecessary confusion.
- Do not place your navigation bar anywhere except at the top of the page. Another case of leaving the user blind on the site.
- Do not forget to plan for an effective navigation scheme. A particularly egregious error is to ignore navigation links back and forth on Web pages within a Web site.
- Do not use Flash!
- Do not test your page with only one browser. It is absolutely essential that Web sites be tested with all the popular browsers. You will be surprised at the differences.
- Do not have too much content. Do not overdo it. Sometimes less is more.
- Do not leave broken links. This is known as "link rot," and the more rot on your Web site, the less reliable it is.
- Do not ignore links to sites outside your library. This leaves the impression with your students that only information within the library is useful.
- Do not think you cannot alphabetize or annotate lists. These are things we as librarians routinely do, but often do not on a Web site.
- Do not forget to have a link to your library's Web site on the district's homepage. A real must if your Web site is to be useable.

## WEB DESIGN AND THE LAW

In Chapter 5, copyright issues with relation to the Internet were discussed. While not all of these apply equally to school library Web sites, as Kennedy says the more you know, the less likely you are to get in trouble. Those of us who have worked with Web page design and construction have probably violated copyright law in some way. Just as a review, the copyright holder has five rights granted by law:

1. The right to reproduce the copyrighted work.
2. The right to prepare derivative works based on the work.

3. The right to distribute copies of the work to the public.
4. The right to perform the copyrighted work publicly.
5. The right to display the work publicly.

Copyright issues and the Internet remain somewhat murky with several key issues not yet adjudicated. Most of us have looked at what we consider to be good Web sites and, following the old adage, "why reinvent the wheel," have borrowed content and graphics from the site. Unfortunately most of us did not ask the Webmaster's permission and may have received a letter or e-mail asking either credit be given or that the content be removed from the Web site.

Many of these unresolved issues deal with links and images, and there are a lot of corporate lawyers waiting to tell you to "cease and desist." Unfortunately many educators feel if an image is used for educational purposes it falls under fair use and is not subject to copyright law. Two examples should banish the notion.

- Your Web page's theme is ideal for some Bugs Bunny images so you find some on the Warner Bros. site and copy them for use on your Web page. Warner Bros. attorneys will send you a polite but firm letter to cease and desist very soon after the page is posted.
- As a school librarian you want to provide links for your administrators, teachers, students, or even parents to purchase concert tickets without having to use Ticketmaster's site. Again, Ticketmaster lawyers will instruct you to remove the links or face legal action.

Three First Amendment issues can get you in some legal hot water. The first of these is less applicable to school libraries than other types of libraries, but the other two are definitely generic to school libraries.

1. Interactive discussion forums. These are just so full of legal issues that the best advice librarians can get is to not do them.
2. Advertising. This is a large issue in most schools. The school district may have a policy addressing this issue, but if they do not, do not advertise for products. You may find yourself in trouble when you need to refuse to advertise a product that would not be suitable to sell over your Web site.
3. Accessibility. This was discussed at some length earlier in the chapter. Suffice to say school districts are bound by ADA guidelines for accessibility on Web sites just as its physical facilities are bound by ADA.

# WHAT SHOULD BE ON A SCHOOL LIBRARY WEB PAGE

Nearly all of the literature has provided lists of things that would be good on a school library Web page. Rather than summarize these lists or recreate these lists here, it is strongly recommended that you explore the Web to see what is out there that is good (or bad for that matter). Also a 2004 article from *Learning & Leading With Technology* by Donna Baumbach, Sally Brewer, and Matt Renfroe titled "What Should Be on a School Library Web Page?" may be useful to aspiring Webmasters. In general, these three authors include the following as possible items on a school library Web page:

- Online Public Access Catalogs. Also include other OPACs your students might have occasion to use such as the local public library, community college, or nearby universities.
- Reference Resources. Include both fee-based and free resources.
- Reference Assistance. You might want to include such things as hints on how to search your catalog or databases.
- Connections to Curriculum Materials. This category is so broad you will have to limit this to the "best of."
- Literacy Materials.
- General Information. Hours, phone numbers, e-mail addresses, etc.
- Dynamic Material. This might be the place you put such things as best-seller-lists or student-produced reviews of new books.

Matthews, in his book *Technology Planning*, provides some more general items about the features on a school library Web page.

1. The Web page should include as much locally developed information on both the page and site as is practicable.
2. The home page should be well formatted and edited. Sloppy just does not get it.
3. The page or site should be easy to locate.
4. Access to information on the site should be clear and direct.
5. Consistency is a plus.
6. A browser search engine is found on the home page.
7. Information should be systematic and hierarchal.
8. Each page should be able to stand on its own.
9. Do everything you can to make the page load more rapidly.

# REVISING OR REDESIGNING YOUR WEB SITE

Almost as soon as you have published your Web site you will see things you should change or things to be added. Unless you have too much time on your hands, you will not be able to change or add things at a moment's notice. You will make list upon list of changes you would make. A few general guidelines simplify the revision of a Web site.

- Create a standard template for the entire Web site containing the library name, logo, and a navigation bar.
- Put what your users want on the Web site as opposed to what you want.
- Check your text information.
- Do not use generic education clip art; do use .alt tags.
- Use dark text, light background.
- Have monthly dynamic information.
- Put things on your Web site that cannot be found anywhere else.

## INTRANETS

School librarians are often asked to participate in the creation of a school district intranet, a Web site created by the school district and limited to employees of the district. It is typically only available inside the district's firewall. The construction and use of a school district intranet has several benefits. The intranet may do the following:

- May eliminate paperwork. This may be chimerical; things that promise this rarely do.
- Can be used to create a "best practices" forum or blog.
- Can allow for the creation of blogs or discussion groups to share problems and successes.
- Can be used as a news outlet.
- Can be used to provide effective search tools.

Chapter 7 introduced the concepts of the school library Web page and the school library Web site. While there was a great deal of information in the chapter, the reader must remember that the chapter only introduces Web pages and Web sites. If more detail is required, there are several books that cover in detail the creation of Web page and Web sites. Also, many educational institutions offer credit and noncredit classes in Web page creation. Chapter 8 will move beyond the creation of Web pages and sites to digital libraries. A digital library offers the full range of library materials and resources electronically.

## RESOURCES

Baumbach, Donna, Sally Brewer, and Matt Renfroe. "What Should be on a School Library Web Page?" *Learning and Leading with Technology* 32, no. 1 (2004): 46–55.

Burke, John J. *Neal-Schuman Library Technology Companion: A Basic Guide for Library Staff.* New York: Neal-Schuman, 2004.

"Evaluating Websites." Multnomah County Library. http://www.multcolib.org/homework/webeval.html (accessed May 28, 2009).

Gordon, Rachel Singer. *The Accidental Systems Librarian.* Medford, NJ: Information Today, 2003.

Janowski, Adam "Instant Web: Just Add Content," *School Library Journal* (January, 2005). http://www.schoollibraryjournal.com/.

Jurkowski, Odin L. "School Library Website Components." *Tech Trends* 48 no. 6. (2004): 56–60.

Jurkowski, Odin L. *Technology and the School Library: A Comprehensive Guide for Media Specialists and Other Educators.* Lanham, MD: Scarecrow, 2006.

Kennedy, Shirley Duglin. "Web Design that Won't Get You into Trouble." Information Today. http://www.infotoday.com/cilmag/jun01/kennedy.htm (accessed May 27, 2009).

Kochtanek, Thomas R., and Joseph R. Matthews. *Library Information Systems: From Library Automation to Distributed Information Access Solutions.* Westport, CT: Libraries Unlimited, 2002.

Matthews, Joseph R. *Technology Planning: Preparing and Updating a Library Technology Plan.* Westport, CT: Libraries Unlimited, 2004.

Minkel, Walter. "Remaking Your Website in Seven Easy Steps." In *The Whole School Library Handbook*, edited by Blanche Woolls and David V. Loertscher, 192–193. Chicago, IL: ALA, 2005.

"School Library Web Site Development Tutorial." Iowatown School Library. http://krueger.uni.iowapages.org/tutorial.html (accessed May 27, 2009).

Valenza, Joyce. "A Webquest About School Library Websites." Wikispaces. http://schoollibrarywebsites.wikispaces.com (accessed May 27, 2009).

Walbert, David. "Best Practices in School Library Website Design." LEARN NC. http://www.learnnc.org/lp/pages/969?style=print (accessed May 27, 2009).

Warlick, David. "Building Web Sites That Work for Your Media Center," *Knowledge Quest* 33, no. 3 (2005). *MasterFILE Premier.* EBSCO. April 22, 2009. http://search.ebscohost.com.

Wohlleb, Jennifer. "Twelve Essentials of a School District Website." *The School Administrator.* (May 2006). http://www.aasa.org/publications.

# QUESTIONS FOR RESEARCH AND DISCUSSION

1. Your principal has given you the responsibility of preparing a policy insuring that the school Web site and all of its content pages are accessible under ADA guidelines. Prepare a policy that could be followed by a school district and also prepare a short presentation for parents explaining the policy.

2. Prepare, test, and publish a school library Web site either for your own school or for a school you are familiar with. Be sure that you use the guidelines provided in this chapter and that you test it on several browsers.

3. Research the Internet and locate six Web sites, three of which you consider to be good and three you consider to be poor. Construct a presentation for your class showing these Web sites and describing the case for or against each Web site.

# 8

# *Digital Libraries*

This chapter and the following chapter are closely related. In Chapter 8 we will address the concept of the digital library and its potential impact on the school library. We will discuss what it is and how it fits in the scheme of education in the twenty-first century. In Chapter 9 the topic will be online materials for the school library. In truth, that chapter's subject could easily substitute the words "digital library" for "school library," and you could easily see the continuum we will be following. You have digital libraries and you have online (read electronic) materials as pieces of that digital library.

A good starting point for the discussion of digital libraries is a definition. Unfortunately no organization or individual has been able to arrive at a definition of digital library everyone has agreed on. Kochtanek, in his book *Library Information Systems*, defined a digital library as one (a library) providing services in a digital realm (239). Unfortunately, while many school library students have used Kochtanek as a textbook, this definition of a digital library is probably not what we are looking for. Digital libraries are also called several other things, such as virtual libraries, electronic libraries, and perhaps even libraries without walls. These terms are similarly lacking precision.

In our experiences as school librarians, many of us have had some experience with the digital/virtual/electronic library when we constructed library Web sites that allowed our students and staff to access and use some or many library resources. As described in Chapter 7, it could be as simple as a Web page only available in school with a link to the catalog or it could be as sophisticated as a complete Web site with access beyond the OPAC to a myriad of other electronic resources. One has only to visit many school library Web sites to see the variety of digital libraries that are currently available.

## CHARACTERISTICS OF DIGITAL LIBRARIES

While not defining the digital or virtual library per se, Kochtanek did enumerate three characteristics considered to be the base of digital libraries (240). First, a digital library is a collection of texts, images, or data that has been digitized. This should give us pause because this does not sound much like the digital library we think of. We do not think of digitizing texts, or pictures, or data; we think of the digital library as a place to go to other Web sites, not a repository for digitized collections. In a sense both of these are correct when early digital libraries were collections of links to other data sources. Second, a digital library should have a system to index and navigate or retrieve information. Third, a digital library should have at least one specified community of users.

Let us consider two examples of digital libraries. The first is the World Wide Web piece of the Internet. Do not forget the Web is only one part of the world's largest network, the Internet. At any rate the Web could be considered the world's largest digital library, although many would disagree with the assessment because there is really little organization to the Web.

The second early digital library was begun in 1971 at the University of Pennsylvania and was called Project Gutenberg. Gutenberg still exists and is a collection of print materials no longer protected by copyright, digitized, and put in the public domain. An example of the type of material available would be the collected works of William Shakespeare. Other worthwhile items digitized by Project Gutenberg are a wide variety of local history materials.

A current, and much more controversial digital library, is Google Books. The search engine company Google has contracted with many of the nation's largest libraries to digitize their collections and make them available in the pubic domain. This entire concept has been challenged in the courts, and the outcome is far from certain.

The third characteristic of digital libraries is the community of users for the digital library. When one considers this characteristic, it is almost self-evident. Even the most basic school digital library has a group of users, the students and staff of the school. No matter what the digital library, there are or should be users for it.

From a theoretical viewpoint, there are considerations that must be dealt with when a librarian is constructing a digital library. This is not just the usual colors, fonts, and appearance issues, but rather issues cutting to the heart of visual libraries.

- An enormous number of digitized texts are available. Which ones will you use? How will you use them? Will you provide links to where they currently reside on the Web? Perhaps most important of all is while there is the huge number of digitized books out there, are they what you and your patrons will want, need, and use?

- Tools have been developed that allow retrieval of networked information. Do they allow you and your patrons to retrieve this information? A prime example of this is e-books. Thought to be the technology development that would end the printed book as we know it, it proved to be something less than that. The biggest issue is that most e-books require an e-book player, and these are proprietary. The Kindle, Amazon's wildly popular e-book reader, is limited to books available in the Kindle format.
- Copyright issues are associated with almost all digital content, whether digitized or obtained from subscription databases. Will your students and teachers keep in mind that fair use does not exclude educational institutions from copyright law?
- Standards are in place for interoperability. Will this be a big issue for the school librarian or is a technology coordinator available and knowledgeable so that you and he or she can discuss the unifications of standards on the digital library you create?
- The design of the digital library should be user-centered. While there are a lot of nifty design things you can do, do they support the user or make it more difficult for the user?
- Creating and maintaining a digital library requires a tremendous administrative commitment. Do you have the skills and the time to do it? If you waver even the slightest bit on this, you might give the digital library a second thought.
- Funds must be available for the digital library project. Will you have sufficient funding to do this? In today's educational funding arena this is as key as all of the other considerations combined. If the funding for the digital library project is not available it will never succeed.

## DIGITAL LIBRARIES AND ONLINE EDUCATION

Five years ago this whole discussion of library services for online education was one properly for postsecondary education. No more. Cyber schools, digital schools, whatever we would like to call them, are growing all over the country and are stunningly successful. Just bear in mind that the largest university in this country is one with a broad online presence, the University of Phoenix.

Online education will be discussed in some more detail in a subsequent chapter, but it is pretty obvious that if public schools are going to provide this online education, then there is probably some equity, if not legal reason, to provide digital library access. In reality this fact obviates any excuse school librarians might have for not providing access to materials electronically. If your school district provides distance education then there is a concurrent obligation to provide online library services. What is provided is within the purview of the school administration and school librarian, but there should be the same level of access to distance education students as there is to face-to-face students.

## DIGITAL LIBRARIES VERSUS TRADITIONAL LIBRARIES

From the time I was in library school at the University of Pittsburgh until I retired, the works and ideas of Blanche Woolls and other outstanding school library educators stayed with me. The school library was to be the center of learning in the school. We all struggled to make this so, and numerous studies have shown the value of an effective school library program in the total educational picture.

Many dedicated school librarians worked hard to deal with one major dichotomy. While the school library was to be the center of education in the school, there were times and issues that sometimes made it unavailable. Many of us had after-school hours, purchased multiple copies of often-used materials, and even permitted reference materials to circulate. That still did not change the fact that the school library and all of its resources were not available seven days a week, twenty-four hours a day. The solution to this issue comes from David Loertscher in his article "The Digital School Library: A Worldwide Development and a Fascinating Challenge." He proposed that every school library in the world would construct and deploy a Web page that would be "the central hub of information essential to every student and teacher" (109). In effect, he was saying this Web page would be the starting point for all information searching.

Loerscher further stated this information system would be an intranet in the school rather than be available on the Internet. Essentially, this means the system would only be available within the school district's firewall and it would not be available from home 24/7. As mentioned earlier, there is a requirement for students, particularly in a distance education environment, to have access to library resources. This precludes the concept that this information system can be effectively used only as an intranet; it must be available on the Internet, and there must be home access to all parts of the system.

While it is pretty obvious to today's user that the digital library must be available through the Internet rather than just through school intranet, Loertscher makes several strong justifications for just this. It is up to the school librarian to make the call as to what is the best system for their school.

# DIGITAL CONTENTS: GENERAL CONSIDERATIONS

Again, Dr. Loertscher's article gives us a general starting point and some unique perspectives as to the digital content that is required for an effective digital library. At the very center of the digital library would be the core collection. This would closely resemble the core collection in a nondigital library and would provide the tools necessary for the majority of the information needs of school library patrons. Many states have provided excellent core collections such as that provided by the Pennsylvania Power Library, available to all public and school libraries in the state.

The second component of a digital library collection would be those materials related to the curriculum of the school. Of necessity this would differ from school to school but might include curriculum-related e-books and databases, subject specific reference materials, and any other digital materials supporting the curriculum of the school. It goes without saying it is in this phase that the contents of the digital library would begin to diverge.

The divergence becomes even more significant as you move into what Loertscher calls the "elastic collection." This is an innovative idea that would give the school librarian control over the contents of the digital library at any particular time. In this concept, school libraries could "rent" materials for the period of time when they are needed. The renting could range from expensive, extensive reference materials needed for only a few weeks for research to large numbers of copies of newly released popular fiction. The whole concept of the digital library could accommodate this "rental" idea: whether vendors would embrace the idea remains to be seen.

As mentioned before, the digital library should be the beginning point of research in the school library and, as such, should be able to be customized by users so they have the resources they need at their disposal. The first category of resource users would need in a digital library would be tools. These might include the following:

- A productivity suite. You are going to have to bite the bullet here and go with MS Office (including PowerPoint). This is the standard.
- A wide variety of graphics programs. Over time students have become more and more proficient with graphics programs.
- Your district's Web creation software. This will be whatever your district has settled on.
- Communication tools including e-mail, chat, and Web 2.0 applications.
- Foreign language translation software.
- Assistive technology for students who require the software.
- Distance education software.
- Appropriate management tools for teachers.

The second category is known as push technology. Early in the days of technology in libraries it was thought push technology would be the panacea for many technology issues, but it never came to fruition. At any rate, the push resources useful in customized environments include automatic notification software and a messaging system. Many educators do not like being contacted by a parent regularly, but it is an integral part of push technology.

The final category is sometimes called pull technology, which is really nothing more than Web search engines that allow users to pull information in from the World Wide Web. Our students, and many of us as well, think the only search engine is Google. Google can be good, but there are other good search engines. You should consider metasearch engines such as Dogpile and search engines expressly designed for elementary school–aged children.

Early in the mid-1990s and the creation of digital libraries, there was some agreement as to the general types of things that should be available on a school library's digital library. These include the following:

- Resources supporting all of the educational needs of your patrons.
- Resources to inform, motivate, or inspire your patrons.
- Information literacy resources.
- Resources to improve the value of the Internet for your patrons.
- Links to other resources on the Internet.

This list is very general, but we must be aware of specific areas and resources.

## DIGITAL CONTENTS: SPECIFIC AREAS AND RESOURCES

As a general rule, digital library content is organized in four categories. These are free Web sites, content developed by the school library, school library–developed interactive services, and fee-based electronic resources (Craver, 18). A digital library can have all of the categories of resources or only one or more of the categories.

- Web Sites. This category can be extensive or as limited as the school librarian would prefer. Early in the digital library creation process, the tendency was to include anything that looked even remotely good. As time passes, however, you become more selective and use only the best sites. Two things are crucial when you are including free Web sites in a digital library. First, make sure the links work! Check them often and get rid of those that do not. Second, include a brief description of the

Web site. Users are less than eager to click on links with no description. Craver made some suggestions as to the type of Web sites adding value to a digital library.

- Use full-text sites.
- Tailor the reference sites to the age of your students. Reference materials for high school students would differ from those for elementary students.
- Include age-appropriate primary sources. For example, there are a wide range of social studies primary source materials available.
- Provide interactive sites. They give added value to the digital library.
- Include instructional interactive sites for such things as bibliography creation or literacy tutorials.
- Feature visual and auditory based sites (19).

- Locally Developed Material. It would be both great and easy if all you had to do was use existing Web sites in your digital library. Unfortunately this is almost never the case. You will have to construct some things such as library rules. Part of the challenge of the creation of the digital library is making the library-developed content attractive and accessible. Craver has again suggested some specific types of library developed content that might be included.
  - General introductory information about the school library. This is an area that requires constant monitoring to insure the information is timely and accurate.
  - Policies and procedures developed by the library and approved by the governing body.
  - Descriptions of special programs the school library has. This could include such things as reading competitions and special displays.
  - Bibliographies and reading lists. These should include not only those you develop but those used by teachers in the curriculum.
  - Web quests and library skill units. Using templates here can be beneficial.
  - Forms for the faculty to use to request services. This is not as simple as it sounds. Think long and hard before you try to create interactive forms.
  - Reference services and term paper assistance.
  - Your periodical holdings list.
  - Assistance on student and faculty Web site development (20).

- School Library–Developed Interactive Services. Of all of the areas that will be described here, this is the one that will present the greatest challenge to the school librarian. These types of services are difficult to construct and even harder to maintain. They will yield great value but should be approached with caution. The types of interactive services that might be available in a digital library are also suggested by Craver.

- Electronic reference assistance. This generally is most effective as an e-mail service.
- Online request forms. As noted above, the creation of interactive forms is a challenge and should be approached with care.
- Interlibrary loan. This is often handled by a state or consortium program such as Access Pennsylvania.
- Library material requests and hold requests.
- Reservation forms for class or library instruction use of the school library.
- Multimedia booking services (21).

- Electronic Reference Services. This is essentially your electronic databases. They need to be a part of your digital library, and it is an absolute necessity they be available for home access. If your databases are not available for home use, change the databases you subscribe to now! What type of subscription electronic resources should be included in the digital library? Craven again has some suggestions.
  - Your OPAC. While not technically a subscription service, the new OPACs with one stop searching would fall into this category.
  - Periodical databases. If your state provides access to an array of databases such as Pennsylvania's Power Library, your digital library will benefit.
  - Trial subscriptions to databases. You must explain clearly that they are trials and may disappear, sometimes in midproject.
  - Database search services.
  - Online general encyclopedias. Again one or more of these may be provided by the state.
  - Subject specific database such as the American National Biography or SIRS.
  - Educational portals such as Bigchalk (23).

These are pretty basic things to include in a digital library, but as you look at some of the digital libraries that are available, you will see a wide range of types of resources that provide a great deal of value to both your student and adult patrons. Rather than a long laundry list of specific types of sites, just consider the categories of resources that make the digital library more valuable.

- The Arts. Art materials are tremendously expensive and often are not widely used. Arts Web sites can be a real money saver.
- College Information. Do not forget links to financial aid sources and to the College Board site.

- Economics and Business. Tremendous amounts of this type of information are available on the Web. Much of the work of the classical economists is out of copyright and is available digitally.
- Education. This should be a major area and can be of great value to your professional staff, particularly those pursuing advanced degrees.
- Foreign Language and Cultures. This type of information has value for background and reference information for those taking foreign languages. Material in foreign languages is also available.
- Geography. Geography courses are rarely offered in schools today, but geographic concepts are very important in our society. Ask some of your students to name five countries in Asia.
- Government and Politics. Of particular note in this category are the digitized versions of almost any government publication.
- Health, Medicine, and Family. This is a bit of a catchall category, but these resources have value in health and family and consumer science courses.
- History. The range of history primary sources is wide and varied.
- Homework Helpers. The question your students will ask is if these homework helpers will do their homework for them. Just grin and bear it!
- Kids' Links. Make sure they are age appropriate for your students.
- Library Links. This is a resource area in which it is easy for you to go a bit overboard. Only include the best links because they will only be used by you and other librarians.
- Literature. Many good literature sites can be found on the World Wide Web. A good technique is to link items in reading lists to author sites and criticism sites.
- Mathematics. The real test here is to include applicable sites for all levels of math taught in the school but not include things so complex students are beyond their depth.
- Media. What a great category this can be for students! Be sure and include all local newspapers with a Web presence and also other major media outlets such as television and radio outlets.
- Writing. This is also a fertile area for links of value to students. Include dictionaries, thesauri, and other sites such as the Purdue University Owl sites.
- Reference. This will undoubtedly be the largest area in your digital library site. Thousands of sites provide reference information not only to your teachers and students but to you as you respond to reference questions. Be careful here, though, because reference sites come and go with some regularity.
- Religion and Mythology. These resources, particularly those dealing with religion, can be controversial. Review the curriculum for

appropriate topics and review any sites you include in the digital library.

- Science. Again there are a plethora of science education Web sites available. Visit the science section of the Glenbrook North High School (Illinois) Web site to see what a fertile mind can do with science.
- Sports and Recreation. Some suggested resources here might be the Web sites of local professional and college teams, along with links to your school's teams. Recreation links should focus on local recreational opportunities.
- Travel. This is again a broad category that includes travel sites of interest to both students, their parents, and to the school staff.
- Search Engines. Links to search engines should be at a high level in the digital library. At this point it is hard to recommend one over another, but as a minimum Google should be there along with at least one meta search engine. This is a category you can experiment with, adding new search engines as they appear and deleting those that are of less value (83).

## ADVANTAGES OF A DIGITAL LIBRARY

The most obvious advantage of a school library's digital library is simple: materials are available twenty four-hours a day, seven days a week. No more situations with too many classes in the library, it is after 3:30 and school buses are leaving, or the library is closed for testing. The digital library is always available. Loertscher suggested several other advantages of digital libraries in his article "The Digital School Library: A World-wide Development and a Fascinating Challenge."

- A digital library provides a starting point for all research. One of the easiest examples of this concept was in the Hempfield Area High School Library in Greensburg, Pennsylvania. Borrowing from an idea at the Bank Library at Point Park University in Pittsburgh, each student in the library at Hempfield had an Internet-connected computer with a complete range of tools and a workspace. This was the beginning point for research for Hempfield students.
- State and federal requirements are to provide adequate and appropriate educational opportunities for all students. This includes such diverse student groups as those students being homeschooled and those who are incarcerated. The digital library is a positive force in providing these required educational opportunities.
- The digital library is ideal in support of students receiving their schooling using distance education facilities. All distance education providers should provide a digital library to insure equity of access.

- Digital libraries provide excellent opportunities for a broad range of patrons to find appropriate research materials all in one place.
- The access to information is not dependent on the patron being in one location. Theoretically the digital library is available anywhere at any time.
- Digital libraries need not be dependent on each user having a particular type of computer or even a computer at all. Digital library content can be made available through any computing device, even a PDA or a cell phone.
- Digital libraries can be customized so users can have access to what they want and need to use.
- Because of the range of selected resources available through a digital library, it is posited that users will search for and receive more germane information. No more Google searches that yield 10,000,000 plus hits. This is a case in which the instruction the librarian has given in the evaluation of Web sites is important.
- The school librarian is in full control of the selection of materials for the digital library.

## POSSIBLE DISADVANTAGES OF DIGITAL LIBRARIES

The reality of the situation is that there are no real disadvantages to having a digital library. Yes, there are issues with the time and technical expertise required to construct and maintain it, but providing library access on a 24/7 basis trumps other issues. Loertscher pointed out some issues that might arise with digital libraries. They are not disadvantages per se, but they can become problems if they are not addressed.

- Access is really an equity issue. The same issue of access is one that bedevils print libraries. Up until recently it seemed a digital library required a computer to use it. That is no longer true as both PDAs and cell phones can gain access to digital libraries. At one time the goal was to put a computer in the hands of every student. Now it appears providing every student with a PDA or cell phone may accomplish the same thing in a more cost-efficient way. While the change from every student having a computer to every student having a PDA or a cell phone makes equity more economical, it still does not address the basic issue of the haves and the have-nots. Until there is complete equity in education (opportunity, materials, etc.) there will still be serious equity issues.
- Enough, but not too many resources. The whole idea of how many resources are enough and, as a corollary, how much is too much must

be resolved. The author can speak with experience concerning this issue. When I constructed our high school library Web page, in reality a digital library, I went way overboard with resources provided. It became a nearly full-time job just making sure all of the links worked. I am not sure there is a hard-and-fast rule as to how much is too much, but if you find yourself doing nothing but checking links you probably have too many!

- Cut and paste. The concept of cut and paste with relation to the Web and plagiarism was discussed in the chapter dealing with copyright, but the more resources available to students, the more likely they are to cut and paste. It certainly is incumbent on the school librarian with a digital library to provide guidance to avoid plagiarism.

- Google. Will Google still be the main way students will access the World Wide Web? I am not sure there is an answer to this one either. I can well imagine a well-designed digital library being ignored by students because they are so used to Googling. This is not just an issue for students, teachers, and school librarians. The answer is, of course, training in information literacy skills, but it is so easy to backslide.

- Copyright and fair use. This is an area that is still wending its way through the courts. While there was always a conflict between fair use guidelines and copyright laws in education, as we move from print to digital libraries, the legal issues will have to be adjudicated.

- Obsolescence of books. Will books as we know them continue to be used in schools? The question to this is certainly not decided. As long as I have taught at the college level I have always asked my students if they thought print books would disappear. The answer is generally "no," but they often differentiate between books read for pleasure and textbooks or research material. Textbooks and many materials used for reference are already moving to e-book format. Of course I and many others agreed with Lancaster who thought computers would lead us to a paperless society.

- Budget. Budget is what drives all educational decisions no matter how little we like it. As a general rule digital libraries cost more than traditional print libraries. But if you look at a 24/7 digital library, how do you compare those costs with those of a traditional print library open approximately eight hours per day and only nine or ten months of the year?

Digital libraries, discussed in Chapter 8, is a very exciting concept. The ideal digital library will provide all the resources students and teachers will need. The challenge will be to insure that they use the right resources and the best resources. The idea that a digital library is just a few Web sites gathered in one place is wrong: a good digital library should be a well-thought-out collection of Web sites and resources and should combine free and subscription resources. Are digital libraries the future for school libraries? I think so, but only time will tell. In Chapter 9 we will focus on online materials that can be used in the school library, either as part of the library's Web site or as part of a digital library. The resources discussed include databases, e-books, e-journals, the invisible or hidden Web, and Google Earth.

## RESOURCES

Craver, K. *Creating Cyber Libraries: An Instructional Guide for School Library Media Specialist.* Greenwood Village, CO: Libraries Unlimited, 2002.

Kochtanek, T., & Matthews, J. *Library Information Systems: From Library Automation to Distributed Information Access Solutions.* Westport, CT: Libraries Unlimited, 2002.

Loertscher, D. The Digital School Library: A Worldwide Development and a Fascinating Challenge. In Esther Rosenfeld and D. Loertscher (Eds.), *Toward a 21st Century School Library Media Program.* (pp. 108–117). Lanham, MD: Scarecrow Press.

---

## QUESTIONS FOR RESEARCH AND DISCUSSION

1. You are considering constructing a digital library for your school. Your two options are to prepare it as an intranet or place it on the Internet. Prepare a paper evaluating the value of each option, along with a recommendation, for a presentation to your school administration.

2. Using Peter Milbury's school-libraries.net Web page, select three digital libraries you consider to be exemplary. Using a standard Web page evaluation form, evaluate each of the sites and then prepare a report on each site for your class.

3. There were several curriculum areas mentioned in the chapter. Select eight of the curriculum areas and locate five Web sites for each of the curriculum areas of value to a high school digital library. Be sure and include an annotation for each of the sites.

4. Will the book survive as we know it? As a group project in your class examine the current research in this area. Present a panel discussion and prepare a PowerPoint presentation supporting or refuting whether or not the book as we know it will survive.

# 9

# *Online Materials for the School Library*

The two previous chapters discussed two closely related topics: the school library Web page and its natural outgrowth, the digital library. This chapter will address some of the concepts introduced in the previous chapters in a bit more detail. Although the role of the OPAC was discussed in detail in Chapter 6, this chapter will briefly review the role of the OPAC in the context of the school library Web page and the digital library. The evolution of subscription data bases and their importance to the school library Web page is a focus of a section of the chapter. The role of e-books and e-journals in the digital library is looked at in depth, as is the question "Is the book dead?" Many of our students and teachers become frustrated when they are searching the Internet and cannot find the information they want. A trip into the invisible or hidden Web should clarify some of those issues. Finally, we explore two relatively new pieces of online material with great applicability in education—Google Scholar and Google Earth.

Just a word of clarification is needed before we continue. Those of you looking for laundry lists of Web sites will be disappointed, but with good reason. The author does not feel particularly comfortable providing lists of Web sites in this book, for two reasons: First, Web sites can change or disappear. Second, what I like you might not. You need to surf the Internet yourself to find the online materials you like.

## OPACS

It is funny how the topic of OPACs keeps appearing in nearly every chapter of the book. At this point in its evolution, however, the OPAC is the single most important piece of online material your library works with. As we have discussed earlier, the OPAC was, for many school libraries, a first experience with technology. As time passed, it was also the first library program to which your technology coordinator permitted home access.

Today the OPAC has evolved into what some would call "one-stop shopping." Depending on the OPAC, when a student enters a search term, the OPAC can search

- The school's catalog
- The catalogs for all schools in the school district
- A statewide catalog such as the one found in one state, Access Pennsylvania
- The fee-based databases to which the school subscribes, or to which it has access through other resources such as the statewide databases offered in some states
- A group of Web sites vetted for credibility and reliability

In the early days of OPACs, we thought things could not get any better—students could do keyword searching rather than having to deal with Sears or LC Subject Headings. Has some artistry been lost? Probably. Are students more accomplished searchers? Definitely.

## DATABASES

If the OPAC was the first piece of technology the school library possessed, a database of some kind, probably of periodicals, was the second. It seems only a few short years ago that searching for information in periodicals was like a rite of passage. We school librarians tried to jazz up our presentations about the *Reader's Guide to Periodical Literature*, and generally failed to do so. The students hated it, because it was often taught in isolation, with no relevance to their classes. The real crunch would come when students would find periodical articles they could use and then found that the library did not subscribe to the magazine, or that the issue was missing.

Technology brought something new to the school library, the electronic database. A database is defined as a collection of information on one or more related topics. The earliest library databases were certainly not easy to use, and searches were often pricey. The first electronic databases with which most school libraries worked were one of either Orbit, Dialog, or BRS. As an aside, it is interesting to note that Dialog morphed into the Alta Vista search engine.

These early databases were not intuitive and generally required a direct modem (dial-up) connection for access. Also, they came with notebooks full of print material describing the databases that could be searched, and a thesaurus of acceptable search terms. The cost of the searches was so expensive that the librarians, not the students, almost always did the searching.

# THE LEAP TO PERIODICAL DATABASES

As time passed some smart librarian thought, "Why can't we search for magazine articles online?" The technology was there, so the influx of online periodical databases began. Many of the early ones were simply computer-searchable versions of print products. The second step was to provide some link between the bibliographic citations and the full text of the article, even if the library did not actually subscribe to the magazine. Many libraries bought into a system called InfoTrac, which provided a bibliographic citation with a code number linked to a sheet of microfiche. What a step forward! Full-text articles were available without subscriptions.

This technology was rapidly replaced as the Web proliferated in school libraries and provided actual full-text magazine articles that could be saved, printed, or e-mailed. Today the three preeminent full-text periodical databases are Proquest (actually a descendant of InfoTrac), Gale, and EBSCO. There is a cautionary tale here, though, about not providing the customer with what they want. The *Reader's Guide to Periodical Literature*, published by Wilson, owned a virtual monopoly on the indexing of periodical literature for many years. As the online periodical index began to become popular, Wilson moved to provide the *Reader's Guide* online. Unfortunately they were very slow to tie full text to their index.

# ADVANTAGES AND DISADVANTAGES OF ONLINE PERIODICAL DATABASES

What are the advantages and disadvantages of full-text online periodical databases? Over the years, many states have recognized the need for library users to have access to a wide array of databases, including a periodical database. An example of this type of service is the Power Library provided by the state of Pennsylvania to all its citizens, at no additional charge, through public and school libraries. Service is 24/7 and requires only a public library card. Students and teachers may access the system through computer access in their school libraries. However, it is feared that an economic downturn will endanger funding for these programs.

A reader might think this section is superfluous, but as you read the advantages and the disadvantages, you will see that all is not as obvious as it may seem. Here are some advantages to the use of online periodical databases.

- Ease of searching. This advantage is similar to an advantage of OPACs versus traditional card catalogs. With a print periodical index such as the *Reader's Guide to Periodical Literature*, searching is only, generally speaking, by subject headings or author. With online periodical indexes, there are many more search options, with the major improvement being the ability to search by keyword.

- Full text. This is probably the major improvement over the more traditional ways of finding magazine articles. With electronic databases, the full text is there. No longer do we miss that magazine or find an issue is missing. Most of the periodical databases have an option to return only full-text articles—the choice for most researchers unless a complete literature search is desired.
- Additional services. These services are not duplicated by other services, and include the abilities to save articles, print articles, e-mail articles, or—sad but true—copy and paste articles. Some see this as a disadvantage rather than an advantage.
- Accessibility to multiple users. In the "bad old days," if a student wanted to read a magazine article another student was using, he or she waited for the current user to finish. With online periodical databases, an unlimited number of users can access the same article at the same time. In addition, online periodical databases are available for home use twenty-four hours a day, seven days a week.
- Space savings. It is no longer necessary for school libraries to keep extensive periodical back files to satisfy research requests. For many veteran school librarians, this can be a wrenching experience, but personal experience shows back files can be limited to one or two years.
- Cheaper and easier to update. With the *Reader's Guide*, each month a new index volume was received, and at the end of the year a new annual volume was received. This means another volume is reviewed to do a complete search for articles on a particular topic. With online periodical indexes, the update is part of the subscription, and the update is seamless, and generally done on a daily basis.

Even with all of these positive points about online periodical indexes, there are some downsides as well.

- High initial costs. This will be discussed in some detail in the next section, but some administrators and school board members can be put off by the high initial costs. They won't always see it, but the school librarian can point out the broader coverage and lower cost per title.
- Downtime. Even the best computer networks have downtime. Just remember: a print magazine index is only available when the school library is open.
- Searching is easy; browsing is hard. I am not sure today's students see the value of browsing related topics, because they are so used to doing keyword searching, but browsing is very difficult with online periodical databases.

- Loss of information sources over time. The coverage in online periodical databases can change as years pass. Some sources are added, and some will be removed. You cannot control it, but a good technique to counter the negative effects is to keep a running list of titles added or deleted.
- Should you no longer have funds to continue subscription to any database, you will lose all access to those resources.

These are the advantages and disadvantages of online periodical indexes. According to Burke (2006, 111–116) there are several other issues the school librarians must consider:

- Authentication. Typically no authentication other than IP recognition is required to access electronic periodical databases inside the school's firewall. Home access generally requires a user ID and password. Remember: vendors do not want to give their content away.
- Technology requirements. Make sure all computers within the school meet the database's technology requirements. You should also provide the technology requirements to parents in the district.
- Cost. It is unavoidable. Online periodical databases are costly to purchase unless you are able to join a consortium for purchase of databases. Vendors will often negotiate consortium discount prices for online periodical databases. See whether your state provides these types of databases to school libraries at no charge. Many states, including Illinois, Ohio, and Pennsylvania (among others), do this.
- Canceling print magazine services. Canceling the print version of magazines because they are in a full-text online database is an issue all school librarians must consider. Doing this saves money from your print budget and can also save you storage room for back issues. Many school libraries now limit their print magazine subscriptions to what could be considered recreational reading and retain back issues for a limited amount of time. The rub comes when titles are deleted from the database or—worst of all—the funds for the database disappear. This can lead to a situation in which key titles may not be available either electronically or in print in the school library
- Using the OPAC for integrated searching. This issue was discussed in both a previous chapter and earlier in this chapter. If your OPAC does not provide this type of searching, you may want to take a hard look at your OPAC.
- Training and education for school librarians. An online full-text database loses some of its value if it is not intuitive, or if no training is provided by the vendor. Furthermore, you will want to closely evaluate the online help, because this is what most of your students will use.

## MAKING DECISIONS TO PURCHASE DATABASE SUBSCRIPTIONS

Because of the cost of online database subscriptions, as much care should be exercised in their purchase as in the purchase of any big-ticket technology item. Peterson published an article in 2003 titled "Stretch Your Budget! How To Select Web-Based Subscription Resources" that put some form to a process for selecting and purchasing these types of products. She advocated an eight-step process:

1.  Prepare a plan. The plan for the purchase of these products should be considered in your collection development plan.
2.  Analyze the needs of your students, faculty, and administration. In particular, analyze whether the product fits the curriculum. Purchasing a product not based on the curriculum or on standards seriously limits its value.
3.  Analyze the product to determine potential management benefits to your school library. These benefits can range from financial benefits to space savings.
4.  Attempt to link to a consortium for cost savings. Many vendors will offer substantial savings for volume purchasing, and they sometimes offer discounts for extended-term subscriptions. Unfortunately, the school budgeting process often precludes this.
5.  Compare products so that you can see how they will function in your library. A good way to do this is to ask for a trial period. I have always done this, and have found most vendors accommodating. If a vendor did not wish to allow a trial period, it really raised questions about the product in my mind. A table similar to the one developed by Peterson and shown below can help you in your comparison

|  | Vendor 1 | Vendor 2 | Vendor 3 |
| --- | --- | --- | --- |
| Product |  |  |  |
| Technical Support |  |  |  |
| Admin Rights? |  |  |  |
| User Statistics |  |  |  |
| Minimum Browser Requirements |  |  |  |
| Home Access |  |  |  |
| Print/E-mail/Download |  |  |  |
| Training/Tutorials |  |  |  |

6.  Negotiate a purchase price with the vendor. This is a true negotiation, because the vendor wants to sell the product, and you probably have a limited budget to spend.

7. Promote the product to all stakeholders. Demonstrate it at faculty meetings. Send notes about it to people who might use it. Use the product in the teaching process.

8. Evaluate the product. After you have promoted the product and have had people use it, evaluate it. You may think the product fulfills many of your library needs, but closely consider how your users evaluate it. If they don't like it, or if they have issues with the product, perhaps you need to reevaluate it.

## E-JOURNALS

In the previous section, we dealt with full-text electronic periodical databases. In reality, this is the biggest piece of the e-journal pie. The vast majority of research publications that are available in a full-text format are available in these databases, but more sources are available for e-journals. Some of these sources are fee-based, whereas others are free. Often the publishers of journals will provide a Web site with links to both the current issue and—in many cases—some or all of the journal's back issues. These Web sites can be of value but often do not have a search capability, so if you do not have an issue date for an article, you may have to browse issues to find what you are searching for.

## ELECTRONIC BOOKS (E-BOOKS)

According to Church, an electronic book, or e-book, is "a digital version of a traditional print book designed to be read on a personal computer or an ebook reader." What a simple definition for such a large and changing field! Many educators and librarians thought that the e-book would eliminate the need for each student to have a textbook, and perhaps even mean the end of the book as we know it. Neither of these things has happened yet, for several reasons.

When we think about moving away from the traditional one-textbook-for-one-student model to e-books, two issues immediately arise. First, e-books require a computer or an e-book reader to use, and not every student has (or can afford) even one of these devices. Second, the downloading of the e-book requires an Internet connection, and preferably a high-speed Internet connection. Again, some students cannot afford this; some geographic areas do not have access to any Internet connection at all.

Further deterrents to the use of e-books are pictorial content and search capabilities. Many e-books and e-magazines do not have pictures, graphs, or charts. Furthermore, it is not as simple to locate a reference in the Table of Contents or the book's index and then find it readily within the text as it is to do so in a physical book.

In addition to equity of access issues, there is still no single widely accepted standard for e-book readers. Until then, the school librarian is rolling the dice on format. Think of the different video and music formats that have come and gone.

One of the hottest products on the market now is the Kindle. The Kindle is an e-book reader sold by Amazon that uses its own proprietary software. Amazon allows the downloading of books to the Kindle for about $10 a book. This is probably the closest to a standard that exists in the e-book field but the Kindle, although reduced in price from its original $350 to $299, is still a significant expense. Unless a district is going to make a large, long-term commitment to this technology, it is still far cheaper to buy a textbook for every student. Apparently, though, e-books are used much more for nonfiction works than for fiction or recreational reading (Civkin 2005, 95).

We have discussed at length electronic books that require dedicated readers. In this section, we will examine electronic books read using Web sites and personal computing devices. The first three sites we will examine are free sites. Electronic books at these sites are free to download, generally because they are in the public domain.

### Project Gutenberg (www.gutenberg.org)
Contents: Over 15,000 e-books, generally older literature (pre-1923) that is in the public domain
Search capability: Title, author, language
### Bartleby.com: Great Books Online (www.bartleby.com)
Contents: Reference, verse, fiction, and nonfiction in the public domain
Search: Title, author, subject
### International Children's Digital Library (www.icd/books.org)
Contents: Over 600 children's books, in their original language and not necessarily in the public domain
Search capability: Title, author, illustrator, language, publication date

The following vendors provide electronic books for a fee to school libraries. Note that you can purchase the e-books you want, and because they come from pretty standard vendors, school libraries can use purchase orders. These titles typically appear in your OPAC, and a link is there for users to go to the e-book.

### Gale Virtual Reference Library (www.gale.com/gvrl)
Contents: Over 500 reference titles in all curriculum areas, with home access to the works provided
### Greenwood Publishing Group, eBooks (www.greenwood.com/ebooks)

Contents: Over 3,000 books (not all reference), about 10 percent specifically for grades 9–12 (Greenwood now publishes all reference books in both print and e-book format)

**Follett Library Resources Company (www.flr.follett.com)**

Contents: Over 12,000 e-books available to be ordered through Follett's Titlewave feature

**Questia (www.questia.com)**

Contents: Over 56,000 books (most protected by copyright) and over 1 million journal articles

An index is also available (the Digital Book Index, at www.digitabookindex.com) that attempts to provide links to all electronic books.

## INVISIBLE WEB

The Invisible Web is also known as the deep Web, the dark Web, or the hidden Web. The greatest part of the Internet cannot be accessed using subject directories or standard search engines. In the early days of the Internet, certain pages were invisible to browsers and subject directories because

- The pages were in non-HTML format.
- The pages had scripts that contained a ? or other script coding.
- Pages that were generated dynamically by other types of database software.

It has been estimated that there are more than 500 times as many Web sites in the invisible Web than there are in the "regular" (searchable) Web. In real numbers, this means that the Web may have over 550 billion pages, with only about 1 billion accessible (through search engines) in the visible Web.

As a general rule, invisible Web resources fall into one of the following categories:

- Pages that contain dynamic content. These are pages returned in response to a query or accessed through a form.
- Pages not linked to any other pages. This prevents Web crawlers from getting to the content. These are typically single pages users have placed on the Web.
- Private Web sites that require a registration and a password.
- Pages whose content varies by how they are accessed.
- Web sites that limit access to the pages in some technical way.
- Pages only accessible through links created by JavaScript or another computer language.
- Pages created in file formats not handled by search engines.

These categories seem to be invisible in themselves. Perhaps it would be better to say that a great deal of invisible Web content is databases, but that might be overstating it a bit. Sherman and Price (2001, 96–103) put together a list of the "Top 25" invisible Web categories. You would be far better served searching the invisible Web rather than the visible Web if you were searching for the type of information contained in these categories:

- Public company filings. These are documents the Security and Exchange Commission requires to be filed on a periodic basis.
- Telephone numbers. Currency is a major issue when using this type of database.
- Customized maps and driving directions. This was once the exclusive preview of Mapbeast and Mapquest, but other sites—notably Google Maps—now provide this capability.
- Clinical trials. Both for the researcher and the person who wants to participate in clinical trials can be found here.
- Patent information. This is an invaluable site for anyone involved in the invention process.
- Out-of-print books. These sites give librarians and individuals the ability to search for and purchase out-of-print books.
- Library catalogs. There are thousands of OPACs available on the invisible Web.
- Authoritative dictionaries. The range from general dictionaries like Merriam-Webster's to very specialized, technical dictionaries.
- Environmental information. Much more about environmental issues is available on the Web than is available in print sources.
- Historical stock quotes. These, according to some financial experts, have some predictive value.
- Historical documents and images. These items are ideal for education. Many can be found at the Library of Congress American Memory Project (http://memory.loc.gov).
- Company directories. This includes such formerly proprietary information as Hoover's and the Thomas Register.
- Searchable subject bibliographies. These can have great pieces of information for the researcher.
- Economic information. Because much of this information is in databases, it is part of the invisible Web.
- Award winners. From Novel Prizes to Emmy Awards.
- Job postings. These are almost impossible to find on the visible Web. Use Careerbuilder.com or Flipdog.
- Grant information. In periods of economic belt-tightening, these resources can be golden for school librarians.

- Translation tools. Sometimes almost too literal, they continue to improve as time passes.
- Postal codes. These are not only for U.S. ZIP codes, but for postal codes from around the world.
- Basic demographic information. This includes U.S. census information.
- Interactive school finders. These sites try to match qualifications with schools.
- Campaign financing information. The most comprehensive information comes from the Federal Elections Commission (www.fec.gov/finance_reports.html).
- Weather data. Accu-weather, which began as a government Web site, is a strong presence here.
- Product catalogs. Some retailer's Web sites are on the visible Web, but others are on the invisible Web.
- Art gallery holdings. These materials are rarely used in print format in libraries, so digital items can save money.

Above we have listed and discussed categories of information that are generally part of the invisible Web. That still begs the question of when and why one would use the invisible Web. As a rule, you probably would use the invisible Web when one of the following conditions is true:

- You are familiar with the topic and think there is more information available than what you are seeing in the visible Web.
- You have a high level of expertise with search tools, including searching using Boolean logic.
- You don't want millions of hits; you want a precise answer.
- You want all authoritative hits in an exhaustive search.
- You need something that is timely.

Two issues remain with our examination of the Web: first, what is not available in either the visible or invisible Web, and second, what tools will allow you to find information on the invisible Web. First, we consider what is typically not available on either the visible or invisible Web.

- Proprietary databases and information sources. This is only available to paying subscribers.
- Many government and public records. Individual privacy rights often trump the right to know.
- Scholarly journals. High-priced scholarly journals are, for the most part, not available on the Web.

- Full text of all newspapers and magazines. This is changing somewhat, but authors' rights are unclear in this area.

The table below provides some tools for searching the invisible Web. This is adopted from Ian Smith and the reader is cautioned that it may take a combination of these tools to actually find what you are looking for.

| Tool | Description |
| --- | --- |
| Complete Planet | Best used for searching, not browsing |
| Direct Search | Searches in the invisible Web |
| Fossick.com | Over 3,500 specialty databases (mostly academic) |
| Informine | Focuses exclusively on academic resources on the invisible Web |
| Internet Oracle | A form and database search tool |
| InvisibleWeb.com | Over 11,000 specialized databases |
| Webdata.com | A database portal |

## GOOD ONLINE MATERIALS

The final section of this chapter will describe briefly two online tools for expanding the use of your Web page or digital library. By no means should you assume that these are the only good online materials out there. They simply represent two of the best sources of information. You are going to have to search the Web for those online resources that are best used by your students and teachers.

### *Google Scholar*

Google Scholar is an access point that allows your teachers and students to conduct broad searches of the scholarly literature. Google Scholar searches all (or nearly all) academic disciplines and includes peer-reviewed papers, articles, theses, abstracts, and books. The material comes from academic publishers, preprint repositories, professional societies, and colleges and universities. Google Scholar allows the researcher to

- Search many sources in one search
- Locate papers, abstracts, and citations
- Locate entire papers, either on the Web or in your library
- See what is being published in your academic areas of interest

### *Google Earth*

Google Earth is one of those online programs we have all seen, at the very least on news programs when they use the satellite representations to show locations of news events. Its powerful features make it an ideal online resource for students and teachers alike.

Google Earth is an interactive program allowing users to see a 3-D version of geographical locations. It provides an aerial view of the location and increases or decreases the magnification as desired. It also provides the alternative view that is available from Google Maps. Different layers can be added to the presentation to show different information. The program itself can be downloaded and used for free. There are a wide variety of helper applications available for Google Earth to enhance its value in the library or classroom.

Russell Tarr, in his 2006 article in *History Review* entitled "Using 'Google Earth' in the History Classroom," listed several applications:

- "Using Google Earth to enhance history."
  - Using terrains or overlays obtained from the Web. These give students a geographic understanding of historical sites.
  - Using 3-D models. These are beginning to come into more common use as time passes.
  - Tours using flyovers.
- "Obtaining existing resources."
  - Google Earth History Illustrated Community (http://bbs.keyhole.com).
  - Google Earth Hacks: Historical Placemarks (www.googleearth-hacks.com/dict40).
- Aids for creating your own resources:
  - Sketchup: 3D Model Creator (http://sketchup.google.com).
  - Tagzania: Create collaborative tours as a classroom project (www.tagzania.com).
  - Flickr Map: Geotag the photographs of your field trips (www.flickrmap.com).

Chapter 9 addressed the materials that are available online for the school library to use. Chief among these are the databases that the school library subscribes to. An area that is growing rapidly in this category is the use of e-books and e-journals. Only about 10 percent of the Web pages that exist are available using regular search engines. The remaining 95 percent is contained in the Invisible Web. Chapter 10 will expand on the discussion of online resources with the topic of librarian-created online materials.

# RESOURCES

"About Google Scholar." Google. http://scholar.google.com/intl/en/scholar/about.html (accessed June 27, 2009).

Botluk, Diana. "Features: Mining Deeper into the Invisible Web." *LLRX*. http://llrx.com/node/1054/print (accessed June 27, 2009).

Brisco, Shonda. "Internet or Database?" *Library Media Connection* (February 2006): 44–45

Burke, John J. *Neal-Schuman Library Technology Companion: A Basic Guide for the Library Staff*, 2nd ed. New York: Neal-Schuman, 2006.

Church, Audrey P. "E-Book Resources for the School Library." *MultiMedia & Internet@ Schools*. http://mmischools.com/Articles.

Civkin, Shelly J. "E-books: Flash in the Pan or Wave of the Future?" In *The Whole School Library Handbook*, eds. Blanche Woolls and David V. Loertscher, 95–98. Chicago, IL: ALA, 2005.

Craver, K. *Creating Cyber Libraries: An Instructional Guide for School Library Media Specialist*. Greenwood Village, CO: Libraries Unlimited, 2002.

Harris, Christopher. "The Truth about Ebooks." *School Library Journal* (June 1, 2009). http://schoollibraryjournal.com.

"Invisible or Deep Web: What It Is, How to Find It, and Its Inherent Ambiguity." University of California. http://lib.berkeley.edu/TeachingLib/Guides/Internet/InvisibleWeb .html (accessed June 27, 2009).

Jurkowski, Odin L. *Technology and the School Library: A Comprehensive Guide for Media Specialists and Other Educators*. Lanham, MD: Scarecrow, 2006.

Kochtanek, Thomas R., and Joseph R. Matthews. *Library Information Systems: From Library Automation to Distributed Information Access Solutions*. Westport, CT: Libraries Unlimited, 2002.

Lackie, Robert J. "Those Deep Hiding Places: The Invisible Web Revealed." http://robertlackie.com/invisible/index.html (accessed June 27, 2009).

Lamdgraf, Tedd, and Ronald Weaver. "At the Center: The Library in the Wired School." *Netconnect* (Winter 2003): 12–14.

Peterson, Janet Walker. "Stretch Your Budget! How to Select Web-Based Subscription Resources." *Computers in Libraries* (February 2003). *MasterFILE Premier*. EBSCO. April 22, 2009. http://search.ebscohost.com.

Rice, Marilyn, Daphne Johnson, and Michelle Pierczynski-Ward. "Google Earth." (nd): 12–15.

Sherman, Chris, and Gary Price. *The Invisible Web: Uncovering Information Sources Search Engines Can't See*. Medford, NJ: Information Today, 2007.

Smith Ian. "The Invisible Web: Where Search Engines Fear to Go." http://powerhomebiz .com/vol25/invisible.htm (accessed June 27, 2009).

Tarr, Russel. "Using 'Google Earth' in the History Classroom." *History Review* (December 2006): 26–27.

Woolls, Blanche, and David V. Loertscher, ed. *The Whole School Library Handbook*. Chicago, IL: ALA, 2005.

# QUESTIONS FOR RESEARCH AND DISCUSSION

1. Your director of library services has asked you to review different options for full-text online periodical databases. You are currently using EBSCOhost, and there is really no implication that EBSCOhost is not satisfactory—just a desire to see what other options are available. The director wants you to prepare both a position paper and a PowerPoint presentation comparing the three major players in the market: EBSCO, Proquest, and Gale. Use the points developed in this chapter to compare these three products.

2. The superintendent is very interested in the concept of e-books as a possible replacement for print textbooks and print reference materials for the school library. You are less sure the concept is feasible but have decided to compare two things: print textbooks versus e-books and print library reference materials versus e-books. Your comparison should present a frank appraisal of both and arrive at a clear, supportable conclusion.

3. The invisible Web broadens the amount of information to which library users have access. In this question, select a topic of interest to you and other school librarians. Prepare an annotated bibliography of twenty sources you locate on the invisible Web. Be sure to include your search strategy for finding each source.

4. In this chapter, we discussed two "good" online resources: Google Scholar and Google Earth. Locate three other online resources that you consider worthwhile. Prepare a PowerPoint presentation describing each and explaining how you envision the resources' being used in the curriculum.

# 10

# *Creation of Online Materials*

In the previous three chapters, we discussed three topics: school library Web pages, digital libraries, and online materials for school libraries. Each of these topics logically followed the other as we began with the school library's Web presence, moved to the digital library, and examined the types of online materials that can be placed on Web pages and in digital libraries. In this chapter, we will examine and describe different types of school librarian–created online materials. For many school librarians this can be a daunting process, because they lack the skills to create their own online materials. So the school librarian has two choices: gain those skills by attending workshops or taking college courses or approach the technology coordinator and ask him or her to assist you. In the long run, you need to gain the skills to create Web pages, so you might as well gain those skills now.

## CATEGORIES OF ONLINE MATERIALS

Craver, in her book *Creating Cyber Libraries*, separated school librarian–created online materials into two broad categories: content and librarian–created interactive materials. Content developed by the school librarian is in the area of general information. This is among the easiest types of information to create, because it is typically created in a word-processing program and then put into a Web page creation program. Later in this chapter, we will discuss in more detail what might be on content pages.

The second area of school librarian–created content is what Craver calls "digital archives." An example of a digital archive might be a database of digitized historical photographs. The digitized photos are placed on the Web, and their description is placed in a Microsoft Access database that is then linked to your Web page. The final area of content includes school librarian–developed materials such as special databases. These are similar to the digital archives described above, but the database typically consists of links to other Web sites, such as curriculum- or library-related Web sites.

The second category of school librarian–created online materials is interactive services. These have been described briefly in a previous chapter, but I cannot emphasize enough the extent to which the creation of interactive services materials on your Web page or in your digital library requires an extremely high level of skill in Web page creation. If you do not have the required level of skill, you should not attempt to access the services. The same warning is applicable to maintaining interactive sites. They take skill and time. Do not attempt them without both of these things.

Assuming you have the skills described above, what types of interactive services can be made available on your school library Web page? All of these services are typically rendered via e-mail.

1. Electronic reference assistance. Providing electronic reference assistance can, on the one hand, be a great benefit to your students and teachers but, on the other hand, it can be your worst nightmare. If you are committed to providing this service, you had better specifically and visibly post the hours this service is available. Nothing will destroy your credibility more quickly than claiming that you are providing this type of service and then not responding to reference questions in a timely manner. If you are not prepared to make this service available in nonschool hours, be sure to make this clear, or try to find a source, such as your local public or academic library, that does provide this service.

2. Online request forms. This can be a real time-saver for the school librarian, who can spend inordinate amounts of time taking calls to reserve equipment. With an electronic form, the librarian can easily plan for equipment use and provide the requestor with a confirmation of their reservation.

3. Interlibrary loan. Using online ILL forms can also be a time-saver, but many states now provide statewide ILL, and the forms used are proprietary. This is the system used with the Access Pennsylvania ILL system.

4. Requests for books or holds on books and materials. The format for this interactive service would be similar to the procedures for equipment reservation, but in this case the confirmation should not be sent until the librarian has verified that the book is in the library and has pulled it from the shelf.

5. Library reservations. Does a teacher need space in the library? Are computers needed by the class? Does the class need instruction? These are things that are confirmed through an interactive library reservation system.
6. Assistance to teachers with instructional design. Not all teachers, particularly those new to the game, can make good use of this interactive service.
7. Multimedia booking. See the comments for items 2–6.

## A NEW PARADIGM FOR LIBRARY ORIENTATION

In Chapter 9, I said that providing instruction in the use of the *Reader's Guide to Periodical Literature* was the most onerous and ignored instruction provided by school librarians. Running a close second to this is the infamous "library orientation." Too often, it is a canned presentation given to every incoming class, either in person or on videotape. You just are not able to convince students the information provided in the library orientation will be used as long as they are in school. They just roll their eyes and take the "I dare you to teach me something" demeanor.

Try something new with your library orientation next year. Put it on a Web site! While this takes a great deal of work to create, the rewards can be large. You can put whatever you want in the orientation, but if you need some hints, here are some suggestions:

- A description of the library. Not just words but digital photos or digital videos. If you're really brave, include voice.
- A description of the displays in the library. Again, use photographs— but a word of caution here: if you are going to use students in your pictures, be sure you are aware of and are following district policy for displaying student work and pictures.
- A description of and pictures of your computer area. If your district uses an acceptable use policy, you might include it here; students can print it out and have their parents or guardians sign it.
- Information about the copying machine. Of all questions I was ever asked as a school librarian, the most common was, "How do I use the copying machine?" We always demonstrated this in our library orientation, but it was as though we never mentioned it. A great technique here is to put a video in your library orientation showing how to use the photocopier. This is also a good place to begin reinforcing copyright law.
- Interlibrary Loan. This is another one of those things students don't care about until they have to use it. Sometimes ILL forms can be

confusing, so showing correctly completed forms can help the students. Furthermore, students can return to this if reinforcement is needed.

- Equipment. This is a case of a picture being worth a thousand words. Include photographs of the equipment available for student borrowing, and an explanation of how they can actually borrow it.
- Microforms. Do you still use microfilm or microfiche? You probably do if you have back files of local newspapers or magazines. Probably all you need here is a description and picture of the microforms.
- Periodicals. Often popular magazines like *Sports Illustrated* or *Glamour* are the hook to get students into the library. Focus on these magazines in your library orientation and, better still, show some happy students reading them!
- Reference materials. Once you get beyond encyclopedias, students really do not know too much about reference materials. Pick a few of the newest and most attractive reference titles and feature them in your orientation.

I cannot promise that using these ideas or creating an online library orientation will work perfectly for you, but considering the alternatives, it is a good option. The question often arises how to tell whether students have worked through or visited the library orientation. The easiest way is to give a short quiz on the contents of the orientation. The score can then become part of a grade in one of the students' classes. This solves the issue of assessment and accountability.

## MORE ONLINE MATERIALS

The final part of this relatively short chapter will list and describe online materials created by the school librarian. They can be part of the school library's Web site or a part of the digital library. Some of these may appeal to you. No claim is made for the materials list's completeness. Items not mentioned here certainly can be part of the process. These librarian-created online materials must fit in your Web site and page design.

- Basic homepage and its components. In either the school library Web site or the digital library, the majority of the content will be created by the school librarian (or whoever is creating the page for the school librarian). Below are some basic components of that page:
  - The mailing address of the library. This probably does not belong in the banner, but rather should be toward the bottom of the page.
  - The name of the library (i.e., Smith School Library), the name of the librarian, the librarian's e-mail address, and the library's

telephone number. This information might appear in a banner, something like this:

Smith School Library
Tom Jones, Librarian
tom.jones@smithschool.edu
(555) 123-4567

- A listing of the employees and a picture and short biography of each one of them.
- The hours the library is open. Be sure to include before- and after-school hours, and any evening hours.
- Webmaster's contact information. Near the bottom of the page you should include the webmaster's contact information (if you are not the webmaster) and the date the Web page was last updated. It is important that the update information be included; currency is one of the criteria for evaluating a Web page.
- Specific librarian-created content. Many of these items will be placed on separate Web pages. Why, you ask? Wouldn't it be easier to put all of the administrative information in one place? For you it would be easier, but psychological studies have shown that Web page users are loath to scroll through large amounts of information.
  - Mission and library policies. These may be as lengthy or as concise as you see fit. You probably already have them somewhere in a word-processing program, so moving them to an HTML document should be easy. Placing your library's policy on the Web page gives them the "official" look for parents and students.
  - Library news. Has one of the librarians received an advanced degree? Have several of your student library assistants received some academic honor? This is the type of information you should include in library news. A word of caution here. Don't be so ambitious that you commit yourself to changing this information on a daily basis. Once every two weeks, or once a month, is plenty. That said, be sure you do update it on a regular basis.
  - A library calendar and/or schedule. A weekly update is probably okay. It should include what classes are scheduled to use the library.
  - A list of new books purchased by the library. This is a really nice touch. With any bibliography you post to the Web, include a link to information about the author. (All you have to do is make the author's name a hyperlink.)
  - An interactive map of the school library. The interactivity occurs when users move their mouse cursor over an area of the library and a picture of the area appears. If they click on these links, it opens a description of that part of the library.

- A list of equipment available for loan by the library. It may be helpful to include here the procedures followed to borrow the equipment.
- A list of the periodicals held by the library. This should include any periodicals to which you no longer subscribe but for which you hold back files. Include the title, the holdings (1996–present, etc.) and the format for each (paper, microfilm, etc.).
- A link from your home page to your library's OPAC. This is your raison d'être. It goes on the home page.
- Award sites. Include such things as lists of Pulitzer Prize winners and Caldecott winners. Again, the links to information about the authors and about the award itself is value-added content.
- Class resources. This should be a section that is updated frequently. It should include items gathered for a specific teacher or class that is working with the librarian.
- Homework assignments. Teachers should be encouraged to put their homework assignments on your Web page, and you should establish links to information to help students complete the assignments.

In sections one and two, a number of librarian-created items that belong on a school library Web page have been discussed. In order to better visualize these, below is a rough schematic of a page on which they might be linked to. This would be a library's homepage.

Smith School Library
Tom Jones Librarian
tom.jones@smithschool.edu
(555) 123-4567
Hours

| OPAC |
| Library Calendar |
| Library News |
| Mission/Policies |
| New Books |
| Magazine Holding List |
| Hardware Available |
| Awards |
| Class Materials |

Library Staff/Webmaster
Last Updated

- Links. It is crucial that your Web site or digital library have links to Web sites used for research, reference, or general information, for the benefit of students, teachers, and parents. Below is a configuration used by the Hempfield Area High School Library (Greensburg, PA) for a number of years to give users an orderly framework for their searching. The order of the elements is not sacrosanct; nor is the table configuration. It must be noted, however, that most Web page creation programs work best with tables.

| Power Library | ACCESS PA | Databases | Reference |
|---|---|---|---|
| Search engines | Web sites | Teacher | Librarian |
| | Subject-specific | Web sites | sites |
| MLA format | Local libraries | Newspapers | Magazines |
| Career/college links | Government Web sites | Weather | Media |
| Health sites | Homework helpers | Research guides | Copyright |

The Power Library is a suite of databases provided by the state of Pennsylvania and includes the most complete version of EBSCOhost, a full-text online periodical database. The content does change as databases are added to or taken out of the Power Library. Access PA is the Pennsylvania statewide catalog of materials that can be borrowed through Interlibrary Loan. At present, all but one of the state's 501 school districts participate in Access PA.

The database section contains links to each of the library's subscription databases. Two other things in this section have proven to be of value: (1) a description of how the database can be used, and (2) PowerPoint tutorials on the use of the database.

The reference links can be as extensive or concise as the school librarian wants them to be. To avoid confusion, we did not include links to reference materials included in either the Power Library section or the Database section. Some hierarchal organization is necessary here. Generally, start with general reference categories (e.g., encyclopedias, dictionaries), then move to subject specific reference sites.

The search engine links should be as inclusive as possible, because everyone has his or her own favorite search engine. Be sure to include a range of metasearch engines, and also tools that can be used to search the hidden Internet. Other really valuable things to include here are links to pages discussing how to most efficiently use search engines.

The subject specific Web sites and the teacher Web sites, again, can be as big or as small as you want. It is crucial that the sites are checked often to ensure that links are valid when users go to them. The links for librarians certainly should be extensive. This is the main site for you and your colleagues to get professional information.

You can substitute APA or Chicago for MLA format, depending on what the standard is for your school. We also included several bibliography creation programs in this section.

We always included links to public libraries, special libraries, and academic libraries in our geographic area for two reasons: (1) our students often used these facilities, and (2) they are a part of our Access Pennsylvania User's Group. This section is a good way to establish good relations with other libraries.

The newspaper and magazine links are visited often. The newspaper links should include all the newspapers in your area. The magazine links should link to the magazine Web site itself, not to an online database. Many of the sites have both the magazine's current issue and some archived materials.

Many of the remaining sections of the table are relatively self-explanatory, except the media links. Our students are so much into the media that you should be as complete as possible. This section might also include ticket outlets such as Ticketmaster.

Chapter 10 continues the material from Chapters 8 and 9, but rather than further examining material from outside sources, it focuses on school library–created materials. Locally created materials include general information materials (such as information about the school library), digital archives (such as collections of local history materials that have been digitized), and interactive materials (such as reading lists with links to author or criticism sites). The locally created materials can be considered the items that introduce school library Web sites and digital libraries, and that also tie the different parts together. Chapter 11 is a key chapter in the examination of technology and the school library. It describes the importance of integrating technology into the curriculum and provides examples of successful integration strategies. It demonstrates that technology is not an end in itself, but rather a tool that is used to implement the curriculum.

## RESOURCES

Craver, K. *Creating Cyber Libraries: An Instructional Guide for School Library Media Specialists.* Greenwood Village, CO: Libraries Unlimited, 2002.

Jurkowski, Odin L. *Technology and the School Library: A Comprehensive Guide for Media Specialists and Other Educators.* Lanham, MD: Scarecrow, 2006.

## QUESTIONS FOR RESEARCH AND DISCUSSION

1. In a documented paper, compare and contrast librarian-created online materials with those available on the Internet. What is the ideal combination of those materials discussed earlier in the book and school librarian–created online materials?

2. Your principal has asked you to liven up your school library Web page by including more locally created material. Prepare a plan for this revision, and include a PowerPoint presentation that is branded for your PTA to explain these changes.

3. Extensive sets of links for your students and teachers to use are some of the best types of local content you can provide. Using the table in this chapter as a guide, locate and annotate at least ten Web sites that you would include for each of the categories you include in your table.

# 11

# *Integrating Technology into the Curriculum*

The role of technology in the curriculum and its integration presents challenges not only to the school librarian, but to the school community as a whole. Parents want it, school boards want it, and administrators want it. With everybody wanting technology in the curriculum, one would think achieving that goal would be easy. Unfortunately, it is not that simple, and the missteps are numerous. All you have to see is the teachers who have put all of their notes into a PowerPoint presentation and then think they have integrated technology into their classes. On top of that, they then read the slides to their students in a darkened room, a practice known as "death by PowerPoint."

Despite great amounts of evidence showing that technology is most effective when teachers integrate the use of technology into the curriculum, many school districts have opted instead to provide what they call "computer class" with "computer teachers." This is particularly prevalent in elementary school situations, where classes go to a computer lab and learn how to "use the computer." In some cases students are taught keyboarding, and in other cases they use different educational software. The class is not taught as part of another class but is often, at least in collective bargaining states, an accommodation for the prep or free period for the classroom teacher.

In secondary schools the computer class often takes a different form, often closely resembling a college microcomputer application class. While this works relatively well in college, all too often the students cannot associate the learning with other situations and have little transfer learning into their classes.

Based on the research that it is better to integrate these technology skills into a class, why not do it effectively even with elementary school students? Isn't it better to teach students word processing skills in coordination with preparing a report for science class rather than preparing a contrived report in a computer class? Further, the concept of "just in time" or "as needed" instruction in technology addresses many issues. Is it important for students to know all parts of a software package, or do they just need to know enough to solve specific tasks? Research shows that the latter is probably the case but other issues frequently cloud the judgment of school districts.

## WHY USE TECHNOLOGY IN THE CURRICULUM?

In addition to the obvious—that technology provides students with the best possible educational experience—four reasons follow as to why integrating technology into the curriculum is a good idea. First, using technology in the educational process motivates students. Our students today are considered the digital native generation, and it is probably so that students will do better in class if they are motivated—and they are more highly motivated if they are able to actually use technology in their classes. To reiterate, reading your notes from a PowerPoint presentation is not an example of integrating technology into the curriculum, nor is it motivating to students.

Second, the integration of technology into the curriculum can provide unique applications for the use of technology which may include different pieces of technology. Take, for example, the opportunity to view video clips to emphasize a point in social studies class. The opportunity for students to use a software program such as PowerPoint to create a presentation is a definite step forward for students in the elementary grades.

The third reason why integrating technology into the curriculum is a good idea is that it supports new approaches in instruction. If one looks at Madeline Hunter's theories, in the past the teacher was "the sage on the stage," an individual who imparted information to the class. Such teachers spend most instructional time lecturing. In contrast, using technology in the teaching process can help teachers to be the "guide on the side," allowing them to be constructivist teachers, with the students taking a more active role in the construction of their own education.

The fourth reason is that using technology to support teaching helps make teachers more productive, and production is expected of teachers today. Using technology can help accomplish both of these goals. By keeping students more motivated and providing the students with better educational opportunities, teachers can do more instruction and therefore become more productive.

# ATTRIBUTES OF INFORMATION-AGE SCHOOLS

As early as 2001, research done on the efficacy of using technology in the educational setting showed trends still true today. This research identified some attributes of information age schools.

- These schools provide interactivity in different venues. It might be e-mail, instant messaging, or participating in video conferencing. These are all interactive experiences students and teachers can utilize in any number of different classes. Just think of the educational value added if students can actually interact with experts in the field they are studying.
- These schools offer much self-initiated, student-centered learning, with the students often forming the question to be investigated. This returns us to the idea of the "guide on the side" in project-based learning or problem-based learning. In these cases, the students, with input or guidance from the teacher, formulate or frame the question to be investigated or solved.
- The teacher becomes a guide or facilitator, rather than an information purveyor. Rarely do you walk through the halls of an Information-Age school and hear teachers lecturing to a class of possibly bored students. Instead you will find teachers who are facilitating instruction, using the technology as a tool in the learning process rather than an end in itself. No computer classes or computer teachers here!
- The library is the center of learning, and the school librarian is a central participant in the learning process. This is explained over and over in the library literature. Furthermore, as we have discussed in this book, the school librarian is not only the instructional leader of the school, but also the technology leader of the school.
- Instruction and learning are continuously evaluated. When this research was done, in 2001, there was not yet the strong push for assessment in schools that there is now. Progressive schools even at that time were intimately involved with assessment, and not just at the end of a unit. Assessment was done on a continuing basis.

These schools look different from schools in the past, and perhaps this is a reason some administrators fear them. Modern schools are not quiet; learning here is a noisy activity. Furthermore, most classrooms do not have a regimented look of rows of desks facing forward. Classes work in groups throughout—even out of—the classroom. Students are coming and going from the classroom to the library as freely as they need.

We have stated this before: in order for technology to be effectively integrated into the curriculum it must be a tool, not an end in itself. Technology can be used to help you construct an effective presentation. It is not the goal to teach you, other teachers, or students how to use the presentation software.

## APPROACHES TO INTEGRATION

In the first two sections of this chapter, we have talked about two things: first, why the integration of technology into the curriculum is good, and second, what some of the characteristics of Information-Age schools are. In this section, we will look at some general techniques that can help the teacher who wants to move toward integrating technology into the curriculum.

The first approach to integration of technology into the curriculum is teacher collaboration and team teaching. Integrating technology into the curriculum works really well in cross-discipline units. This all becomes possible with the school librarian leading the collaborative process, and it allows great opportunities for technology integration. Preparing reports using a word processor, making posters, and creating Web pages are just the beginning. The opportunities for collaboration and technology integration are myriad, as you will see when we look at some examples of technology integration in the subject disciplines further along in the chapter.

Flexibility in scheduling can really help integrate technology into the curriculum. Some things just do not lend themselves to the standard 45-minute class period. Some schools have attempted to solve this issue with block scheduling, but in the end, just remember that good teaching is not bound by class periods. You must be flexible yourself, and you must encourage your teachers to be more flexible!

Of all of the approaches to the integration of technology into the curriculum, the one that most generally comes into play for school librarians is information literacy. It has been called different things at different times, but instruction in information literacy provides great opportunities for students to work with technology tools as they learn the information literacy skills they will carry with them not only throughout their school years, but also throughout their lives.

In the elementary school students begin doing basic research with electronic resources and then use that information to prepare reports, bibliographies, or presentations using the most appropriate computer software. At the secondary level, the research skills become more complex, as do the computer applications. More types of technology are added to the equation, such as streaming video and primary source documents. By the time students who have well-developed skills in information literacy leave for their post-secondary education or enter the job market, they will also have a level of technology skills that enables them to compete both in their postsecondary education and in their career.

Throughout this chapter we have emphasized that although instruction in the use of software is a key technology skill for students, this is one of the areas that almost begs for technology integration. Earlier in this chapter, we discussed the idea that teaching the use of computer software in isolation provides little transfer learning, and that students taught that way take little with them. It is far better to train students to use computer software in a curriculum integration situation than to try to teach those skills in isolation. When students are doing a project-based learning experiment and have to do a presentation to their class, this is a good moment to teach them how to prepare effective presentations with a computer presentation program such as PowerPoint. Not every bit of teaching about or with technology has to be planned down to the last detail. Take advantage of those teachable moments!

Again, we have skirted the issue of research as an approach to the integration of technology skills into the curriculum. Research has always been the backbone of library and curriculum instruction. Traditionally the "big" push in research is the ubiquitous research paper as part of the English or social studies curriculum. No matter what the discipline, in today's education, research involves technology. Other than finding information in books located using the school library's OPAC, the vast majority of student—and, for that matter, teacher—research is done using technology in the form of electronic resources. Furthermore, once the research is done using electronic resources, it is presented in the form of some other electronic format. After all, no students are using typewriters to produce reports now!

Many types of electronic resources can be integrated into the research aspects of the curriculum. For example, students can access e-books, video, graphics, and audio from the World Wide Web. Students can participate in audio and video conferencing with other students or with experts in their field of research to broaden their research knowledge.

Although it must be obvious that I do not believe in teaching technology skills in isolation, I will admit there are a few times when teaching a "computer class" can be a beneficial educational experience for students. For example, office technology students who are preparing for office jobs probably do need to learn software applications completely, because they just don't know what part of the software package they will have to show expertise in on that first job interview, or in the job itself; another example is those classes in software programming.

Another opportunity for the integration of technology into the curriculum comes with collaborative learning. One of the skills most employers want their prospective employees to bring with them is the ability to solve problems using a collaborative approach. One of the important aspects of collaborative learning is the ability to use whatever tools are available to solve the problem. If the problem solvers have the tools but do not know how to use them, they have a responsibility to learn to use the tool effectively. Many teachers do not like collaborative learning because of the assessment issues as the students try to become experts in doing little and still getting a good grade. I believe we must follow some of industry's lead in assessing collaborative output. If industry can do it, education can also.

Students can also gain experience using both Flash and animation techniques as ways of integrating technology into the curriculum. These and other more sophisticated programs and techniques students can use at great profit. Furthermore, they are technology skills students will be able to carry with them into other venues.

Another approach to the integration of technology into the curriculum is to work with interactive programs. These types of programs are motivating, and they encourage students to learn more in an environment they like. The use of interactive programs in the curriculum is a challenge for teachers. It takes some levels of training and a lot of trial and error in order to use these effectively in the classroom.

## INTEGRATING TECHNOLOGY INTO THE CURRICULUM

Doggett, in her work *Beyond the Book: Technology Integration into the Secondary School Library Media Curriculum*, discussed in some detail the pros and cons of integrating technology into the school library curriculum. Although some of her points were covered earlier in the chapter, there is value in considering each in turn. Again, even though the points deal specifically with the school library curriculum, they are equally applicable to the general school curriculum.

### Pros

- Integration of technology into the school curriculum facilitates school to career preparation. As discussed earlier, employers are looking for employees who can work in collaborative, team situations, and who are technologically able. This does not mean that students have to be able to work with every piece of software, but rather that they must show a capacity to learn to use the technology they will have to work with in their jobs. A comparison can be drawn to the 1960s and 1970s with education for several types of engineers. Employers looked at education in engineering as providing a base of learning and a capacity to be trained; the employer then provided the specific training required for the particular job.

- The second positive point for the integration of technology into the curriculum is a change of paradigm in the mode of instruction. Since the dawn of public schools, instruction has been nearly the same. A student from the 1850s who was placed in a public school 100 years later would find nearly the same type of instruction, called by some "chalk and talk." The spread of technology has changed that. Teaching with technology requires a whole new skill set for teachers; most traditional teaching methods are not particularly effective in teaching with technology.

- Using technology as a tool in teaching opens new avenues for assessment. Many educators have been less than thrilled about "No Child Left Behind," but the movement caused administrators, school boards, teachers, and administrators to examine new methods of assessment. Schools are moving away from paper-and-pencil assessments, tests, quizzes, and papers toward what is called "authentic assessment." When students are presented with real-life problems and scenarios, alternative types of assessment can be devised using technology that fairly evaluates student progress. Does authentic assessment easily lend itself to assigning better grades? Perhaps not, but it provides a more realistic evaluation of performance.

- The use of technology in instruction can enhance students' critical thinking skills, a much-desired and seldom-achieved goal of instruction. Part of the issue has always been that measuring critical thinking skills is very difficult using traditional assessment methods. Using a technology-infused curriculum can provide some measure of critical thinking skills not available previously.

- The use of technology in the curriculum also gives students wider access to information. Technology has significantly increased the amount of information available to students. Whether it is magazine articles, video snippets, or even pieces of music, information has become much more available to students. Take for example the use of general encyclopedias. In the past, there were a finite number of volumes available, and if more than one student wanted to use the same volume, one used it and one waited. With access to electronic encyclopedias, any number of students can use the same information at the same time. Also, the electronic resources are available both at home and at school, twenty-four hours a day, seven days a week.

- Of all of the advantages of technology discussed so far, one of the most desirable is the currency. When instruction takes place in a more traditional setting the instruction is typically textbook-based. With this type of instruction and the use of textbooks, the information is at least two years old, because of the time cycle involved with writing textbooks. The use of electronic resources is current to the point that full-text magazine articles are often available electronically before they are available in print.

- The final advantage Doggett espouses for the integration of technology into the curriculum is one discussed before—motivation. Students today are part of the digital generation and are motivated by the technology they can use. Technology appeals to students who are visual learners as well as those who are tactile learners. A major problem for educators is always motivating students. How much more interested students become when their lesson is introduced with a piece of streaming video or part of a music video! These are the types of motivational devices technology can provide for twenty-first-century students and teachers.

### Cons

With all of the positives we discussed above, one would think the integration of technology is an open-and-shut case. It is completely understood the pros far outweigh the cons. However true that is, people with budgetary responsibility do not always see technology or the integration of technology into the curriculum as essential enough to assign sufficient funding. Let us examine some of the cons, as described by Doggett.

- In the short term, it is more costly to integrate technology into the curriculum than not. In the long run, however, it is less costly—but most school districts have to pay in the short term, not wait for the long term. Furthermore, many parents, teachers, and students expect the latest and greatest technology, and this is sometimes beyond the means of school districts.
- Closely related to the first item is the issue of rapid change. Change in technology is inevitable, and it is not cheap. When a new operating system is introduced, it means that every personal computer has to be updated to maintain a commitment to currency.
- Compatibility issues bedevil school districts all across the country, and those types of issues can wreak havoc with school district budgets. Sometimes one platform is a better choice for certain tasks than another platform is. From an educational standpoint, having both platforms is sound, but from a business or budgetary standpoint, it is a problem that is very difficult to deal with.

- The best plan for integrating technology into the curriculum can be completely hamstrung by a lack of training. Too, too often we throw technology at teachers with the expectation that they can learn how to use it in their "spare" time. Some can do it, but it is not fair to expect people to learn new technology with no training.
- Equity, equity, equity. Does every student in your school have a computer? Does every student in your school have access to high-speed Internet? Do all of your teachers have access to computers that can be taken home? These are just a few of the equity issues for which educators must account when assessing the effectiveness of the integration of technology into the curriculum.

## STRATEGIES FOR INTEGRATION OF TECHNOLOGY INTO THE CURRICULUM

Our approach to examining strategies for the integration of technology into the curriculum will be twofold. First, we will examine the strategies that facilitate this integration; then we will look at different subject disciplines and see what techniques would work within each of the disciplines. The author makes no claim that this is an inclusive list, only that they seem like good techniques and either have been demonstrated as being successful or show promise. It is incumbent on you, the educator, to try things to see what works. Feel free to modify and adapt any of these ideas in the classroom. Keep in mind that technology is such a dynamic field that many of these strategies could be completely outmoded by the time you read this book.

### *Productivity Software*

Some of the most commonly used strategies facilitating the integration of technology into the curriculum are built around productivity software. Productivity software comes in a package such as Microsoft Office (which includes different programs such as a word processor [Word], spreadsheet [Excel], presentation software [PowerPoint], and a database package [Access]). Although there are often other pieces in the productivity package such as a scheduling or e-mail packages, the foregoing are the major pieces students and teachers will use. The most likely use is the research paper, for which, as mentioned earlier, a database finds citations, the word processor handles the text, and (depending upon the topic) Excel creates charts of data to add to the text. Productivity software gives the student the ability to use each piece of the software in conjunction with the other pieces or independently. In addition, there is file compatibility which allows files created with one piece of the software to be imported into other pieces and then worked with interactively. For example, a student can create a spreadsheet and a chart from the data and then place it in a PowerPoint presentation. Any changes made to the data in the Excel spreadsheet are automatically updated in the chart, and also in the PowerPoint file. What a powerful lesson this can be in "what if" analysis.

Another example of the use of productivity software used to integrate technology into instruction is in the creation of visual book reports by elementry students. The students read the book and then use technology in the school library to research the author. The output uses two applications of the productivity software: the word processor to prepare the report about the book and the author, and the presentation software to prepare a visual presentation of their report.

Another example is the research paper, which is done at several different levels. The students use the technology in the library to do research on their topic and the word processor to prepare the final research report. This instruction also includes the use of the grammar checker and the preparation of the paper's documentation.

### Games and Simulation

Educational games and simulations have been around the education field for many years and represent some of the first educational software available for students. Gaming has become so popular with children and teens that it has almost taken on a life of its own and eliminated the educational side of things. Even so, there are great educational games and simulations available in many disciplines and at many grade levels. Using these tools in the elementary grades can really motivate and also provide much-needed reinforcement for skills building.

At the secondary level there are also many games and simulations available for students. Who can forget, in the early days of Apple computers, working with the math and social studies concepts in Oregon Trail? I don't think anyone ever made it to the West Coast alive! Oregon Trail still exists, albeit updated with all of the bells and whistles students today want. Sim City is another game secondary students still find not only motivating but educational without being overpowering.

Many textbook companies now offer online simulations with their books, such as MyITLab, MyMathLab, and MyWritingLab. Games and simulations continue to fill a need in the educational technology picture, as they are valuable reinforcers.

### Drill and Practice

Drill and practice technology goes back to the first days of the use of technology in schools. Drill and practice technology can be either linear or nonlinear and can give students valuable practice with such basic skills as reading and computation. The best drill and practice software provides reinforcement when a student responds incorrectly, rather than indicating that the student is incorrect. The software provides the student with more practice in the concept when he or she is not successful. One question has always arisen in my mind about drill and practice software. It may be a good motivator for some students, but in many cases, the same thing can be accomplished with a paper and pencil at a much lower cost. If you are not careful and you do not encourage your teachers to be careful here, you end up with technology for technology's sake.

## Tutorials

In some ways, tutorials are similar to drill and practice in their purpose. Modern tutorials can not only motivate the student but can break difficult concepts down into step-by-step interactive demonstrations. For example, one of the more difficult concepts for students when using Excel is absolute and relative referencing. Tutorials demonstrating this concept typically have four distinct parts. First, the concept is demonstrated for the student. Second, the student is given the opportunity to demonstrate understanding of the concept. Third, if he or she is still having difficulty with the concept, he or she is directed to a part of the tutorial to practice the concept, and finally has the opportunity to show mastery of the concept. Tutorials have improved and are continuing to improve since the early days of technology and provide students with the opportunity to master difficult concepts independently.

## Discussion

No matter what their form, chat, IM, or the Web 2.0 discussion forums such as Facebook or Twitter are all a true conundrum for educators. Many school districts have bans on interactive discussion for several reasons, generally because it is a nonproductive use of technology or because it allows students a chance to share things surreptitiously with other students.

While acknowledging all the negatives, there are good, cogent, educationally sound reasons why students should have access to interactive, real-time communication. For example, one of the key things in AP history courses are the DBQs. The DBQs assess the ability of each student to work with historical sources in multiple forms. Teachers can conduct moderated chat on a regular basis to give students the opportunity to discuss their ideas, as I have seen happen in a classroom. The key to discussion types of technology is for the teacher to control the discussion, not just let it go with no direction.

# DISCOVERY, PROBLEM SOLVING, AND COOPERATIVE LEARNING

These concepts are called many different things, but they essentially describe the same process, generally done in a cooperative, or team environment.

- A problem is posed. This can come from the teacher, or the students can frame it.
- The students research the problem. They discover what kind of information is available, and check to see whether tentative solutions already exist.
- Students formulate a hypothesis. They do this in an effort to solve the problem or answer the question.
- Students test their hypothesis.
- Students present the results of their problem-solving activity.

This is an integral part of constructivist instruction and can be designed to use technology in all aspects of the project. There are many Web sites available under such diverse topics as project-based learning, problem-based learning, discovery learning, problem solving, and cooperative learning.

# DISCIPLINE-BASED IDEAS FOR INTEGRATION OF TECHNOLOGY INTO THE CURRICULUM

This is really the fun part of this chapter for the author. In this last section there is a listing of things that work when you want to integrate technology into the curriculum. I have seen these things work, and you can easily adopt and adapt them to your needs or change them as you see fit. They are not inclusive, but they definitely work.

## *Elementary*

While many good elementary programs are available for educational use—far too many to try to list—teachers can begin to work with students using productivity software.

- Short reports using online library resources and a word-processing program.
- Animated presentations using streaming video inserted in PowerPoint presentations.
- Basic scientific research and preparation of reports summarizing their findings.

- Information literacy and library instruction. This can and should begin in kindergarten and should continue through the elementary school years.
- Math drill and practice using technology. Many programs are available; pick the ones providing the most motivation.
- Reading software keyed to primary readers. The best of this software should be interactive.

### Secondary

#### English

- Video book reports, including information about the author
- Student created tutorials showing research paper creation steps
- Senior projects
- Just-in-time technology tutorials, as needed
- e-Books and e-journals, to supplement subscription electronic databases
- e-Books, so multiple students can read the same book

#### Mathematics

- Use of manipulatives.
- Use of many Web sites, such as Dr. Math, to assist students with difficult concepts
- Use of graphing calculators
- Use of productivity software, especially Excel, to work at charting data
- Finding data online that then can be manipulated in Excel

#### Science

- Use of Web sites such as the Glenbrook South High School science Web site to explore more about scientific concepts
- Use of special hardware such as scientific probes to perform actual scientific experiments
- Use of simulations to recreate scientific conditions that are too dangerous to recreate in schools
- Use of productivity software to prepare lab reports
- Use of proprietary software bundled with science textbooks to amplify scientific concepts

#### Social Studies

- Primary research performed using electronic collections such as the *Official Records of the Civil War*

- Distance learning equipment used to interview experts in fields such as economics and psychology
- Use of interactive real-time conversation to gain insights in AP history classes
- Work with digitized local history sources
- Prepare local history projects, such as Planet Smethport

*Foreign Language*

- Prepare virtual art museum tours
- Communicate with residents in foreign countries to polish language skills
- Use productivity software to present information about foreign cultures

*Music*

- Use of electronic music sites to gain knowledge about music history
- Use of proprietary software to design band routines
- Creation of a departmental Web site

*Tech Education*

- Use of CAD and CAM software to complete problems and projects

Chapter 11 summarizes the importance of integrating technology into the curriculum. Technology should not be an end in itself, with computer classes and computer teachers, but should be integrated seamlessly into the curriculum. For example, the research paper process involves a combination of writing, research, and technology skills that take the student from the idea for the research paper to the completed, word-processed paper, and even to the preparation of a presentation about the research. The only possible places where technology should be taught without curriculum integration are in programming classes and in classes that prepare students to use specific software applications as part of vocational preparation.

Chapter 12 is an exciting chapter that includes the Web 2.0 applications students are expert with. It includes blogs, wikis, social networking, podcasting, virtual conferencing, online education, and virtual sites with avatars.

## RESOURCES

Burke, John J. *Neal-Schuman Library Technology Companion: A Basic Guide for the Library Staff*, 2nd ed. New York: Neal-Schuman, 2006.
Doggett, Sandra L. *Beyond the Book: Technology Integration into the Secondary School Library Media Curriculum*. Edgewood, CO: Libraries Unlimited, 2000.

Johnston, Michelle, and Nancy Cooley. *What We Know about Supporting New Models of Teaching and Learning through Technology*. Arlington, VA: ERS, 2001.

Lever-Daffy, Judy, and Jean B. McDonald. *Teaching and Learning with Technology*. Boston, MA: Pearson, 2008.

Robbyer, M. D., Jack Edwards, and Mary Anne Havrilick. *Integrating Educational Technology into Teaching*. Upper Saddle River: Prentice Hall, 1997.

Rosenfeld, Esther, and David V. Loertscher, eds. *Toward a 21st Century School Library Media Program*. Lanham, MD: Scarecrow Press, 2007.

Smaldino, Sharon E., Deborah L. Larother, and James D. Russell. *Instructional Technology and Media for Learning*. Upper Saddle River, NJ: Pearson, 2008.

## QUESTIONS FOR RESEARCH AND DISCUSSION

1. Select an academic discipline and design a unit plan using and integrating technology into the instruction. The unit should encompass seven to ten instructional days and should be complete enough to include outcomes and educational objectives. Be sure the technology piece is not teaching technology skills in isolation.

2. Using the unit plan created in Problem 1, create the lesson plans to accompany the unit plan. They may be created in the format your school district uses or, if you are a student, in the form accepted by your college.

3. Analyze the arguments for and against the use of computer teachers and computer classes instead of the integration of technology into the curriculum.

# 12

# *Web 2.0 and Related Technology*

## INTRODUCTION TO WEB 2.0

Most of us have read or heard references made to Web 2.0, and we wonder what the difference is between the World Wide Web and Web 2.0. We wonder what we will do with Web 2.0 when we have not yet even mastered the World Wide Web. Be certain—your students are familiar with Web 2.0, and you need as much knowledge as you can get about what Web 2.0 is and how it can be used in school libraries.

In this chapter we will discuss several topics relating to Web 2.0, including a new concept called Library 2.0, social networking, blogs, wikis, video conferencing, course management systems for distance education, and virtual sites using avatars. But bear in mind that much that we will discuss is only slowly being implemented into school libraries. It is no longer the future, but as yet its potential is only slowly being tapped.

Kroski, in her book *Web 2.0 for Librarians and Information Professionals*, defined Web 2.0 as a participatory Web (1). Each of the topics listed above is participatory, even interactive, to some degree. From an educator's viewpoint, Kroski offers several reasons why Web 2.0 is valuable.

- Web 2.0 is valuable because it makes the creation of content easy. More and more, blogs and wikis are taking the place of Web pages. Although blogs and wikis are certainly not as sophisticated as traditional Web sites, they are a "quick and dirty" way to create valuable content.
- Web 2.0 applications generally feature some level of interactivity. Today's students are motivated by the use of interactive technology, and Web 2.0 supplies this.

- Web 2.0 applications provide great opportunities for collaboration. What could do it better than a wiki that students can create and modify? Can this be dangerous? Yes. Can it be beneficial? Again, yes.
- Web 2.0 gives students and educators the opportunity to participate in knowledge communication (8–9).

One of the crucial components of the communication and interaction associated with Web 2.0 is its openness. It is this very openness that scares educators. The issue of interactive, real-time communication, discussed in previous chapters, is an essential part of Web 2.0. If school librarians are to move forward with technology, we must embrace new concepts, not fear them.

In 2005 O'Reilly coined the term Web 2.0 and described it as "the second generation of Web based tools and resources" (O'Reilly). He listed some of the characteristics of Web 2.0 and how it contrasted with the World Wide Web of the time:

- Web 2.0 moved from single-computer Web access to connections with many computers. This is an essential point if collaboration is to be successful.
- Web sites are changing into dynamically created online resources—wikis, for example.
- Some closed systems (Windows, Mac OS) are being replaced by open systems and software (Linux). However, this is an area of technology into which many school librarians hesitate to venture unless they are true techies.
- Web 2.0 moves beyond single users publishing things once to focus on content that is continually added to through user participation.
- Web page authors and creators are shifting from single-person efforts to strong, collaborative, consensus-building efforts.
- Web 2.0 is not about data storage, but about networking and socialization.
- Web sites are no longer just visited—you contribute information to them.
- Organizations shift from being standards-based (taxonomies) to being user-based (folksnomies). Users themselves attach the words to the data (O'Reilly).

## LIBRARY AND SCHOOL LIBRARY 2.0

As we have moved toward the interactivity of Web 2.0 in the general Internet arena, so, too, have librarians moved toward a new definition of technology, called Library 2.0. This move was initially described by Casey in 2006. In effect, it outlines a framework for expanded Web services in the library. Manes, in his 2006 article, defined Web 2.0 as "the application of interactive, collaborative, and multi-media Web-based technologies to Web-based library services and collection." He further theorizes that Library 2.0 has four elements:

1. Library 2.0 is user-centered. The user participates in the creation of dynamic content.
2. Library 2.0 collections have video and audio in addition to text.
3. Library 2.0 has both synchronous and asynchronous communication opportunities available for Library 2.0 users.
4. Library 2.0 is always innovating and changing.

Earlier in this discussion, we said that school librarians must be ready to move forward into this collaborative, interactive world of Web 2.0 and Library 2.0. How many school librarians are moving forward, and how many are going to wait and see? Time will tell.

### Social Networking

Social software has emerged as the part of Web 2.0 with which most people are most familiar. This includes Facebook, MySpace, and this year's "application du jour," Twitter. Our students are in love with these applications; they are the chat of the twenty-first century. In most school districts, all these social networking applications are blocked from student use. As has been said before, there are good, cogent educational reasons to use these applications. If they are integrated into the curriculum and controlled, they can be educationally sound.

Lamb and Johnson in their articles about social technologies characterize social networking as a "computer-mediated communication environment that connect people for cooperation, collaboration, and information sharing." These social networking applications encourage interaction. This is the thing students really like. They are social people, but seem to prefer the computer-mediated environment much as people who used the chat feature did. Second, they give students the opportunity to give and receive feedback. This is important in the assessment of the educational experience. Students and many adults seem to really like the connections they form through social networking.

In this article Lamb and Johnson pointed out several reasons for the popularity of social networking software:

- Providing a sense of activism. Our twenty-first-century students have a very strong sense of activism, and social networking software plays to this strength.

- Providing a sense of belonging. Using social networking applications allows students to overcome social shortcomings. There are no "jocks" or "nerds" in social networking.
- Allowing students to contact one another as they see fit. Social contact is a 24/7 activity.
- Freedom. This is why many school districts bar the use of social networking applications—some students do not deal with freedom as well as others.

### Twitter

The social networking application currently the most popular is Twitter. Twitter is a free messaging service that allows people to send and receive short messages, no more than 140 characters, called tweets. Tweets can be sent using a computer, mobile phone, or PDA. If you want to see what others are saying, you "follow" them (subscribe to their posts). Many tweets are pretty basic ("I watched the Pirates game tonight"), but the article "Twitter for Librarians" suggested some good ways Twitter could be used in a library:

- Twitter allows librarians to keep in touch with colleagues and friends.
- Twitter helps a school librarian to stay on top of the latest technology. This is really important in those ubiquitous one-person school libraries.
- Twitter allows librarians to stay on top of the news; major news sites such as CNN participate in Twitter.
- Twitter allows you to learn about conferences you may want to attend virtually. Some high-tech conferences participate in Twitter.
- Twitter allows school librarians to participate in impromptu question-and-answer sessions.
- Twitter allows school librarians to find out a little bit about their colleagues. Twitter tweets can be very revealing.
- Twitter can be used as a quick notepad. This is not its primary purpose, but it is a useful one.
- Twitter can act as a low-level online reference service.
- Twitter can be used to announce new library services. Your teenage and tech-savvy people will love this service.
- Twitter is the ideal vehicle for posting new materials lists.
- Twitter can send students with Twitter accounts notifications about materials ready for them or about overdue library materials.

### Blogs

Blogs, or "Web logs," broadly defined, are online logs whose posts are arranged in reverse chronological order. These posts can be text, graphics, video, or audio, but most are text. The use and creation of blogs is an example of one-to-many communication and can have significant educational benefit as students collaborate to create and add to journals and gather reactions to postings. Although blogs have traditionally been associated with computers, they can be accessed using any mobile computing device.

McPherson's article "Literacy Links: School Library Blogging" discusses the use of blogs in school libraries and advances several reasons for the use of blogs in that environment. Generally speaking, in the school library, blog issues are raised; others respond using the blog. This is a bit of an oversimplification, but it is the general idea.

School library blogs can be used to promote the skills of reading and writing. Not only are these skills key for our students, but encouraging them also helps show the school library's relevance to state and federally mandated testing. A way blogs can be used in the school library to encourage reading and writing is to encourage students to post book reviews to the blog. This would then allow students to reply or comment to the review. The process of creating book reviews encourages both reading and writing, as does the process of commenting on or adding to the review.

In this same vein, using the book review and commenting scenario should also at least encourage students' critical thinking skills. There is certainly opportunity for this in the actual creation of the review, but it seems as though it is also strongly fostered in the responses to the review. If this can actually improve critical thinking skills it is a great benefit, but the proof will be in the empirical evidence that using a blog in this way will actually accomplish this aim.

Using a school library blog may improve the students' information literacy skills. Often either the beginning posting to a blog or the responses to the posting call for some bit or amount of research. By doing this research, students should improve their information literacy skills.

### Wikis

The other powerful collaborative tool gaining in importance as Web 2.0 has increased in popularity is the wiki. A wiki (whose name is a Hawaiian word meaning "fast") is a set of Web tools that allow two or more people to work together to create something in a virtual environment that is greater or better than what they could have created individually. McPherson held that wikis make the writing process a social process.

Joyce Valenza, the school librarian at Springfield Township High School in Pennsylvania, and a well-known school library technology expert, holds that wikis allow users to "freely create and edit Web site content using their browser" (129). For students, the wiki quickly becomes a tool for students to write—particularly, collaboratively—and receive comments and feedback in a nonthreatening environment. What a boon for those whose reading and writing skills may still not be fully developed!

Certainly the best known wiki is Wikipedia, an online encyclopedia featuring over 3 million articles of various lengths and levels of detail written by users around the world. As one reads the literature about wikis and Wikipedia in particular, two extremes are evident: some feel that Wikipedia is an excellent beginning reference source, and others doubt its reliability from beginning to end. The biggest issue with Wikipedia arises because anyone, no matter their qualification, can post entries to Wikipedia or make changes to what is already there. This open atmosphere can cause trepidation among educators, and many colleges and universities will not accept references to Wikipedia in material submitted at those institutions.

The article "An Info-Skills Workout: Wikis and Collaborative Workout," by Annette Lamb and Larry Johnson, examined the characteristics of wikis and how they can profitably be used in education. With wikis, the emphasis is on authoring. Rather than just adding, wiki users are encouraged to submit new information and new things. Wikis typically use open editing tools, so there is little or no financial stake in them. Lamb and Johnson noted some characteristics of wikis.

- The content of the wiki is original and therefore unique. Users are writing and posting original stuff to the wiki.
- The wiki provides a space for collaboration that is both free and open. Collaboration is one of the keys with a wiki, as it is with many Web 2.0 applications.
- A wiki allows open editing. This is sometimes good, and sometimes bad.
- A wiki is simple to use. The tools used to create the posting are very similar to those found in most word processors. The learning curve is not high.
- Wikis are constantly evolving. Again, this is not always ideal, but it is a fact of life with wikis.

Lamb and Johnson also enumerated several possible applications for the use of wikis in education. Wikis can be used as an aid for collaborative problem solving. This is especially true if the collaboration does not need to be synchronous.

- A wiki provides for collaborative research. Each member of the team can easily post his or her research to the wiki.

- A wiki provides for collaborative writing. Wikis take advantage of students' providing feedback to other students about their writing using the wiki.
- A wiki is a great journal or notebook. For example, in a class, students can post to a teacher's wiki about what is being presented in class.
- The wiki is a great vehicle for the creation of electronic portfolios. This is one place where allowing others to edit or change could be a very positive factor.
- A wiki can act as a portal, or a starting point for learning.
- A wiki is not only a good device for collaborative research, but also a good place to aggregate research to share it with others.
- A wiki, with enough contributions, can be a very good study guide.
- A wiki is a low-cost substitute for expensive video conferencing equipment.

A school librarian has many good educational reasons to use wikis in the school library, but wikis have a few negatives as well (2007, 133–139). First is the open nature of a wiki that allows entries to be edited at will. This can be a dangerous thing with students unless it is closely monitored. Second, wikis can broadcast some students' difficulties reading and writing, something detrimental to their self-esteem. Finally, many, many students do not feel comfortable with the collaborative process. School librarians and teachers may have to do a great deal of handholding to get students to get full value from wikis.

### Podcasting

Nearly every one of our students in the digital generation has an audio player such as an iPod. An iPod is the perfect vehicle to provide content to students and is easy to access and inexpensive. By definition, a podcast is a "digital recording of a radio broadcast or similar program made available on the Internet for downloading to a personal audio player" (Eash). Most of our students don't look to iPods for much more than music, but there are some really good educational applications for podcasts.

Although MP3 files have been around for some time, podcasting and RSS (Really Simple Syndication) mean that users no longer have to surf the Web to find MP3 files for download. The use of Web feeds allows iPod users to subscribe to and download audio content.

The article "Podcasting in the School Library: Part 1: Integrated Podcasts and Vodcasts into Teaching and Learning," by Lamb and Johnson, presented two discrete sections, the first presenting some criteria to consider when evaluating available podcasts:

- Learner needs. Does the podcast meet student needs exactly? It does little good to provide podcasts beyond what the students can understand.
- Content. Is the quality of the content high-quality? Is the person who did the podcast an expert in the field? Can his or her qualifications be verified?
- Technical quality. What is the technical quality of the podcast? Too many high-quality files are out there to use those that are not.
- Design. Is the podcast well designed?
- Instructional quality. Does the podcast meet high standards of instructional quality? You would never want to make a podcast available to your students if it were not of good instructional quality.

Lamb and Johnson then presented some possible uses of podcasts in the educational setting. Many of these applications refer to products available on the Web, although it is certainly not beyond the ability of most educators to create simple podcasts.

- "Collaborative projects."
- "Discussion of current events." Many of these types of podcasts are available from news sources such as CNN.
- "Government documents or government events." An example might be a speech by a prominent government official.
- "Interviews." Many various interviews with the famous (and infamous) are available for download.
- "Conflicting issues." Again, many of these are available from news organizations.
- "Teacher lectures and notes." This is particularly valuable for students who are absent from class, because these are available 24/7.
- "Programs." Does your school hold band or choral concerts? Broadcast them as podcasts for download.
- "Reviews." Let's take the program idea a step further. If your school is having its musical broadcast as a podcast, add reviews from satisfied viewers. A great way to increase attendance!
- "Virtual tours." We have all been to museums that provide taped tours of their collections. Take it a step further and provide a podcast (2007, 163–170).
- Library promotion. This is an especially good vehicle for promoting reading and advertising new books.
- Exemplary student products. This can include papers, posters, or even student-produced podcasts.

- Public information. Keep the public informed of what is happening in the school and school library through the use of podcasts.
- Professional development. The podcast is a great way to provide professional development programs in small snippets and can be available to teachers at any time.

School librarians can follow a few simple steps to create podcasts. These steps may vary depending on your library situation, but they are pretty universal.

1. Figure out what hardware and software you will need for the podcast.
2. Know what content will be on the podcast.
3. Practice the podcast until you are comfortable with it.
4. Record the podcast.
5. Test the podcast, and redo the parts you are not happy with.
6. Publish the podcast.
7. Publicize the podcast to make sure people know about it.
8. Evaluate your podcast, and make the next one better!

### Virtual Conferencing

Although virtual conferencing was more important five years ago, it has been passed by other collaborative applications; only two approaches to this technology are discussed here.

The first type of virtual conferencing could be considered a "value-added" chat. Our students have been using chat for some time, but using mini-cameras can add value to synchronous chat. This kind of virtual conferencing is easily done but requires some equipment investment.

The second type of virtual conferencing involves the use of very expensive distance education equipment. Although the equipment is expensive, many school districts purchased the equipment using grant monies. In many school districts, the school librarian is responsible for the equipment and preparing and executing the video conferences. If that is part of your responsibilities, then be advised: This equipment is often prone to failure. Be prepared for technical difficulties, and be ready with a backup plan. Furthermore, because this technology requires transmission lines from one site to another, technical assistance is required at both locations to make sure the system is functioning. The cost of the transmission lines may be prohibitive, even if the school district owns the proper equipment.

### Course Management Systems

Class management systems are just one piece of the distance education process. Online education is the educational phenomenon of the twenty-first century. What can be better than instruction available twenty-four hours a day, seven days a week—not just 10 a.m. on Monday, Wednesday, and Friday? All the student needs is a computer.

Since the first days of distance education, there has been a K–12 presence. Initially, the thrust was to provide education opportunities to students who would not otherwise have them. For example, Purdue University has provided online instruction in calculus to students at Indiana schools too small to provide such a level of mathematics instruction themselves. In other areas, school districts have formed consortia to provide instruction in subjects without sufficient enrollment to support a teacher in each school.

The picture has changed significantly today. Digital schools are everywhere, providing high-quality education to such diverse groups as confined children, homeschooled students, and children unable to function in a traditional school environment. Two examples of statewide digital schools are the Florida Virtual High School (www.flvs.net/Pages/default.aspx) and the Pennsylvania Cyber School (www.excelatpavcs.org). Now, however, distance education is being decentralized to regional educational agencies, and even to individual school districts. Today, course management systems must be considered.

Course management systems are software systems that allow teachers to manage online instruction. In addition to full online courses, they are also used to manage blended and face-to-face courses. Using a course management system ensures that all communication and learning tools in one place share a navigation system.

Choosing the right course management system can be a real challenge. The commercial systems are quite expensive but often provide a "finished look" that open systems lack. Another decision to make is whether you will host the system, or whether it will be hosted on the vendor's servers. Here are several of the most popular course management systems:

- Angel Learning (commercial K–12 system)
- Moodle (a free, open course package, widely used in the K–12 environment)
- Sakai Project (free and open-source, but high-end, used by many large universities that produce their own systems)
- Think.com (free, offered by ThinkQuest)
- Blackboard (commercial, Web-based, and the most popular system at all levels; Blackboard now owns WebCT)

In 2005, Kathy D. Munoz, Bart Bos, and Joan Van Duzer ("Blackboard vs. Moodle: A Comparison of Satisfaction with Online Teaching and Learning Tools") conducted research at Humboldt State University comparing and contrasting Blackboard and Moodle—a commercial system with an open system. The results are interesting:

| Blackboard | Moodle |
|---|---|
| • Partly owned by Microsoft<br>• Licensed worldwide<br>• Average license = $10,000/year | • Free and open-source<br>• Customizable by local programmers<br>• Flexible<br>• Supported by programmers worldwide |

| Advantages | |
|---|---|
| • More polished<br><br>• Better gradebook<br>• Easier to provide feedback | • Announcements more prominently displayed<br>• Easier threaded discussion<br>• Easier to track student activity |

In the end, 35.7% of the respondents favored Moodle, 21.4% favored Blackboard, and 42.9% had no preference.

### *Virtual Sites with Avatars*

The final topic we will discuss in this chapter is virtual worlds and the creation of avatars. A word of warning before we begin: this is not for everybody, and requires a high level of technical expertise.

In virtual worlds, people interact with others who share their interests. In these virtual worlds, students can roleplay, go on virtual field trips, and hold events. When you go into these online spaces, you create a two- or three-dimensional representation of yourself that becomes your persona online. This is called an "avatar"—a virtual version of you.

Well-done social environments, virtual sites, are a good chance to model high technology learning in a safe online environment. Some technology issues must be considered when working with virtual sites:

• Make sure you have enough bandwidth.
• Make sure your applications work with your data projectors.
• Watch to see if software must be downloaded before you can use the application.
• Confirm the skill levels.

Some security issues that must be considered include the following:

• Do not allow students to share private information.
• Help students know the difference between their online and real-life persona.
• Know what is public and what is private.

The concept of Web 2.0 has many exciting opportunities for school libraries, and they must be ready to meet the challenge. Many of the areas discussed in Chapter 12 have been the exclusive property of our students. We must change that and become experts with social networking, with wikis, with blogs, with podcasts, and with all the rest of Web 2.0 applications. In the final chapter, Chapter 13, we will take a look at what the future might hold for school librarians. It is pure speculation—that killer app may still be in the developmental stage!

## RESOURCES

"ABCs of Web 2.0: Avatars, Blogs, Collaborative Wikis: Avatars, Virtual Worlds, and Social Networks." Eduscapes. http://eduscapes.com/sessions/abc/abc2.htm (accessed July 10, 2009).

"ABCs of Web 2.0: Avatars, Blogs, Collaborative Wikis: Blogs, Vlogs, Podcasts, and Web Feeds." Eduscapes. http://eduscapes.com/sessions/abc/abc3.htm (accessed July 10, 2009).

"ABCs of Web 2.0: Avatars, Blogs, Collaborative Wikis: Collaborative Wikis, Documents, and Projects." Eduscapes. http://eduscapes.com/sessions/abc/abc4.htm (accessed July 10, 2009).

"ABCs of Web 2.0: Avatars, Blogs, Collaborative Wikis: The World of Web 2.0." Eduscapes. http://eduscapes.com/sessions/abc/abc1.htm (accessed July 10, 2009).

Achterman, Doug. "Beyond Wikipedia." In *Toward a 21st Century School Library Media Program*, eds. Esther Rosenfeld and David V. Loertscher, 148–153. Lanham, MD: Scarecrow, 2007.

Alexander, Bryan. "Web 2.0: A New Wave of Innovation for Teaching and Learning?" *EDUCAUSE Review* 41, no. 2 (March/April 2008). www.educause.edu/EDUCAUSE+Review/EDUCAUSEReviewMagazineVolume41/.

Bos, Bert, Kathy D. Munoz, and Joan Van Duzer. "Blackboard vs. Moodle: A Comparison of Satisfaction with Online Teaching and Learning Tools." Humboldt State University. www.humboldt.edu/~jdv1/moodle/all.htm (accessed July 10, 2009).

Casey, Michael E., and Laura C. Savastinuk. "Library 2.0: Service for the Next-Generation Library." *Library Journal* (September 1, 2006). *MasterFILE Premier*. EBSCO. July 10, 2009. http://search.ebscohost.com.

Eash, Esther Kreider. "Podcasting 101 for K–12 Librarians." *Infotoday* 26, no. 4 (April 2006). www.infotoday.com/cilmag/apr06/Eash.shtml (accessed July 10, 2009).

Hargardon, Steve. "A Little Help from My Friends: Classroom 2.0 Educators Share Their Experiences," *School Library Journal* (October 1, 2009). www.schoollibraryjournal.com.

Harris, Christopher. "School Library 2.0: Say Good-Bye to Your Mother's School Library," *School Library Journal* (May 1, 2006). www.schoollibraryjournal.com.

Harris, Christopher. "SL2.0: Visioning the School Library 2.0." Infomancy. http://schoolofinfomancy/infomancy/?p=131. (accessed July 10, 2009).

Kroskie, Ellyssa. *Web 2.0 for Libraries and Information Professionals*. New York: Neal-Schuman, 2008.

Lamb, Annette, and Larry Johnson. "InfoTech: An Info-Skills Workout: Wikis and Collaborative Writing." In *Toward a 21st Century School Library Media Program*, eds. Esther Rosenfeld and David V. Loertscher, 132–138. Lanham, MD: Scarecrow, 2007.

Lamb, Annette, and Larry Johnson. "InfoTech: Podcasting in the School Library, Part 1: Integrating Podcasts and Vodcasts into Teaching and Learning." In *Toward a 21st Century School Library Media Program*, eds. Esther Rosenfeld and David V. Loertscher, 162–170. Lanham, MD: Scarecrow, 2007.

Lamb, Annette, and Larry Johnson. "InfoTech: Want to Be My Friend? What You Need to Know about Social Technologies." In *Toward a 21st Century School Library Media Program*, eds. Esther Rosenfeld and David V. Loertscher, 178–183. Lanham, MD: Scarecrow, 2007.

Lamb, Brian. "Wide Open Spaces: Wikis, Ready or Not." *EDUCAUSE Review* 39, no. 5 (September/October 2004). www.educause.edu/EDUCAUSE+Review/ EDUCAUSEReviewMagazineVolume39/.

"Learning Spaces: Course Management Systems." Eduscapes. http://eduscapes.com/ hightech/spaces/course/index.htm (accessed July 10, 2009).

McPherson, Keith. "Literacy Links: Wikis and Literacy Development." In *Toward a 21st Century School Library Media Program*, eds. Esther Rosenfeld and David V. Loertscher, 143–147. Lanham, MD: Scarecrow, 2007.

McPherson, Keith. "Literacy Links: School Library Blogging." In *Toward a 21st Century School Library Media Program*, eds. Esther Rosenfeld and David V. Loertscher, 154–157. Lanham, MD: Scarecrow, 2007.

McPherson, Keith. "Literacy Links: Wikis and Literacy Development." In *Toward a 21st Century School Library Media Program*, eds. Esther Rosenfeld and David V. Loertscher, 143–147. Lanham, MD: Scarecrow, 2007.

McPherson, Keith. "Literacy Links: Wikis and Student Writing." In *Toward a 21st Century School Library Media Program*, eds. Esther Rosenfeld and David V. Loertscher, 139–142. Lanham, MD: Scarecrow, 2007.

Maness, Jack M. "Library 2.0 Theory: Web 2.0 and Its Implications for Libraries." *Webology* 3, no. 2 (June 2006), www.Webology.ir/2006/v3n2/a25.html (accessed July 10, 2009).

Milstein, Sarah. "Twitter for Libraries (and Librarians)." *Infotoday* 29, no. 5 (May 2009), www.infotoday.com/cilmag/apr06/Eash.shtml (accessed July 10, 2009).

O'Reilly, Tim. "What Is Web 2.0? Design Patterns and Business Models for the Next Generation of Software." O'Reilly. http://oreilly.com/Web2/archive/what-is-Web-20 .html (accessed July 10, 2009).

Rosenfeld, Esther, and David V. Loertscher, eds. *Toward a 21st Century School Library Media Program*. Lanham, MD: Scarecrow, 2008.

"Twitter for Librarians: The Ultimate Guide." College@Home. www.collegeathome .com/blog/2008/05/27/twitter-for-librarians-the-ultimate-guide/ (accessed July 10, 2009).

Valenza, Joyce. "Something Wiki Comes This Way . . . Are You Ready?" In *Toward a 21st Century School Library Media Program*, eds. Esther Rosenfeld and David V. Loertscher, 129–132. Lanham, MD: Scarecrow, 2007.

## QUESTIONS FOR RESEARCH AND DISCUSSION

1.  Construct both a blog and a wiki. You will need to research how to do each, and then post meaningful content. Maintain each for one month (longer, if you prefer), and then report back to the class with your results.

2.  Social networking is spreading like wildfire. Research either Facebook, MySpace, or Twitter. Create an account, and also research the application to see how widespread its use is, and what educational applications exist for it. Prepare a fifteen-minute presentation for the class summarizing your findings.

3.  Create a podcast presenting a ten-minute professional development snippet. Follow the instructions for preparation given in the chapter. Present your podcast to your class.

4.  Do research on podcasts relating to your interests or certification. Download three and view (vodcasts)/listen (podcasts) to them. Prepare a presentation for the class summarizing your findings and your evaluation of the podcast.

# 13

# *The School Librarian, Technology, and the Future*

For twelve chapters we have tried to describe technology and technology skills we feel are essential if the school librarian is to continue to play an essential, central role in the school. We have discussed in detail what technology is available and how it can be used in the school library, both from a theoretical and a practical viewpoint. In addition, we have tried to describe key skills and attitudes for the school librarian to be a leader in technology in their school. Is the world going to come to an end if these things don't happen? Probably not, but school librarians' failure to move forward with technology will certainly handicap their position in the school structure.

In this final chapter we will polish up our crystal balls and see what the future might hold for technology and the school library. Technology is dynamic and ever-changing. The noted science fiction writer Arthur C. Clarke noted in 1962 that "[a]ny sufficiently advanced technology is indistinguishable from magic" (Levy 050). Think back to the first attempts at computer classes, when questions about how something worked were often met with the response, "It's magic"—in other words, the answer was far beyond us non-nerds. And now we are trying to see what the future might hold, what killer application is coming down the road, what the next "magic" will be. Although this is our intention, almost anything noted as a possibility when this book was written may be a reality as you are reading it.

## TECHNOLOGY FOR TEACHERS

A change is coming in instruction, and as we school librarians put on our teacher caps, these are some of the things we might see in the future:

- Interactive instruction. The move to interactive instruction has already begun as we become less of "sages on the stage" and more the "guides on the side." Interactive instruction involves the integration of technology into all aspects of instruction. Only lecturing from the front of room just doesn't cut it anymore.
- Personal response systems. These types of systems are coming at all levels of instruction but now seem most prevalent at the college level. Personal response systems can be as simple as handheld clickers or as complex as computer-supported personal response systems whereby the instructor can monitor an entire classroom of computers and personal response systems.
- Mobile assessment tools. We are really almost there now. Any device with a computing capability, PDA, cell phone—or whatever—can act as a mobile assessment tool.

### Technology for Inclusion

The concept of inclusion (having children of all abilities in the same classroom) seems to be the direction in which education is moving. In order to assure equity for these students, there must be a concurrent move to significantly improve the technology for these students. Although hardware and software are (and have been) available for students with physical and learning disabilities, there must be significant improvement in the technology for these students if we are to ensure equity in the inclusion classroom.

### Technology Innovations: The Twenty-First Century and Beyond

In 2008, Stephen Abram published an article entitled "20 Things to Watch" in *Information Outlook*. In this article, he noted twenty technology trends that he felt would have a big impact on libraries and librarians up through 2013. Even though this article is barely a year old, some of the items he mentions have already become reality:

1. Mobile computing devices. What a soothsayer! One has only to look at the prevalence of iPhones, Blackberries, and PDAs to see how important mobile devices have become. If you do not have a mobile device, you are already behind in technology.
2. GPS systems. These are already installed in most new cars, and GPS devices small enough to fit in a very large pocket are available if you have an older car and want the capability. GPS systems will enable search engines to locate you. The final implications of these devices for education are not known.

3. Open handset alliance (Android). This Google-backed initiative is pushing for all phones to connect using the same standard. With the move to standards across all types of technology, it seems that almost any kind of content can be viewed on a handheld device. It follows that if telephones can be connected using the same standard, then so can other computing devices, all using the same standard.

4. Tagging. This is one of the Web 2.0 applications that has a great potential in determining social relevance in the rankings of search engines.

5. Scrapbooking. Not paper-and-scissors scrapbooking, but the ability to find resources in online full-text databases and then to capture them to your personal computer for later use.

6. Software as a service (SAAS). This uses a server farm to store software. This can save school districts money, and security, backup, and anti-malware costs are significantly reduced.

7. Microblogging. All social networking software now has microblogging features similar to those of Twitter. We have seen the impact of Twitter, and increased microblogging features could cause this to expand.

8. Social content. As we move forward with wikis and blogs, the ability to capture and share this content increases.

9. Social networking. The use of these applications just keeps increasing. School librarians who ignore social networking, and who allow their teachers to ignore it, do so at their own risk, and do a disservice to their teachers.

10. Social networking integration. One step further, this can connect school library Web pages to social networking and tagging sites.

11. e-Books. This topic was discussed in greater detail earlier. The implications for the integration of e-books and other e-content are great for school libraries.

12. e-Book devices. Keep in mind: Amazon cannot keep the Kindle in stock. As other vendors develop readers and ways to access e-books, the cost for the reader will go down, and it may become as economical to purchase the reader and download textbooks. Textbook publishers may find themselves providing parts of their textbooks, rather than a complete text, if teachers do not require all the chapters for all purposes.

13. Personal homepages. We have discussed library Web sites and virtual libraries as being necessary for the school library. The next trend could well be linking library Web pages to personal Web pages.

14. Cloud software. Cloud software is software that is not loaded on local computers but rather is hosted by another server, such as one belonging to Google. Furthermore, documents will not be saved locally, but on servers, as is already the case with Google Docs (http://docs.google.com). It appears that a portion of the upcoming version of Microsoft Office will feature cloud computing. Although the concept is good, there are definite security issues with cloud software.

15. RSS groups and readers. This is a very simple way to read blogs. These new RSS tools will allow the clustering of similar topics.

16. Podcasting and music. As podcasts continue to grow in popularity, companies such as Wizzard Media that gather them for distribution will increase in importance.

17. Streaming media. This is replacing DVDs. Now that the "pipe" is large enough, this is the next way to deliver video.

18. Custom Search and Micro Federation. These are watch services that try to group blogs or databases by subject.

19. OpenID. The ultimate in single sign-on. This system would allow users to have one user ID and password for all things. There are some security issues associated with this. The main one is if the password for single sign-on is compromised, all items in that single sign-on are compromised.

20. e-Learning. The ultimate opportunity for teachers and school librarians to be guides on the side.

This is just a sampling of ideas about where technology is going for school libraries. That being said, these are nothing but guesses about the future. Whatever the future holds, school librarians who have overcome their reluctance to accept technology in all its new forms will remain leaders in helping teachers teach and students learn.

## RESOURCES

Abrams, Stephen. "20 Things to Watch." Information Outlook. www.sirsidynix.com/Resources/Pdfs/Company/Abram/IOColumn_67.pdf (accessed June 27, 2009).

Levy Steven. "Losing the Magic," *Wired* (May 2009):050–051.

Smaldino, Sharon E., Deborah L. Lowther, and James D. Russell. *Instructional Technology for Media and Learning*, 9th ed. Upper Saddle River, NJ: Pearson, 2008.

# QUESTIONS FOR RESEARCH AND DISCUSSION

1. Considering the various roles of a school librarian, try to predict ways in which technology will enhance your responsibilities as a professional. Consider how you will interact with your peers, students, parents, and the community in which you work. Prepare a report of your findings for your class.

2. As a prospective school librarian, what are your present strengths and weaknesses in technology? How do you plan to address these weaknesses? Technology evolves over time, providing users with newer and more creative tools. What are your plans to stay current? How will you continue your professional growth?

# Index

## About the Author

WILLIAM O. SCHEEREN is retired as library department chair from the Hempfield Area School District, Greensburg, Pennsylvania. He is currently a lecturer in education at St. Vincent College, Latrobe, Pennsylvania. Dr. Scheeren holds a Ph.D. from the University of Pittsburgh.